Preserving Modern Landscape Architecture
Papers from the Wave Hill — National Park Service Conference

Edited by Charles A. Birnbaum
Historic Landscape Initiative,
Heritage Preservation Services

D1319080

S P A C E M A K E R   P R E S S

Cambridge, Massachusetts

Acknowledgments

Partial support for this publication was provided by the Graham Foundation for Advanced Studies in the Fine Arts.

Front cover:
U.S. Air Force Academy Air Gardens,
  Colorado Springs, Colorado
  Dan Kiley landscape architect
Photograph by Stewart's c.1958. Local
  History Collection, Pikes Peak
  Library District. Stewart's No. 38-27

ISBN: 1-888931-21-3

Printed by Palace Press International
  in China

No part of this book may be reproduced or utilized in any form or by any means, electronic or mechanical, including photocopying, recording, or by any information storage and retrieval system, without permission in writing from the publisher. Inquiries should be addressed to:
Spacemaker Press®
147 Sherman Street
Cambridge, MA 02140

" The National Park Service (NPS) Historic Landscape Initiative promotes responsible preservation practices that protect our nation's irreplaceable landscape legacy. In partnesrhip with federal and state agencies, professional organizations, and colleges and universities, the HLI achieves its goal by disseminating guidelines for landscape preservation; producing innovative toolsto raise awareness of the general public; organizing and conducting training symposia and workshops; and providing technical assistance for significant properties and districts."

Many individuals contributed to the realization of this conference and its proceedings. For their organizational wizardry and business acumen we are most grateful to Catha Grace Rambusch and Chris Panos at the Catalog of Landscape Records in the United States at Wave Hill. Without their guidance, and the support of Wave Hillís Director Kate French, the National Park Service-Wave Hill partnership would not be possible or as fruitful.

We are also grateful to Dean Cardasis and the James Rose Center, who assisted with the garden tours on the second day of the conference, and Ellen Harrington and Pam Havert at the American Society of Landscape Architects, who provided the original graphic design for the conference. Special thanks also go to Mary Daniels, head of Special Collections at Harvard Universitie's Frances Loeb Library for making the recently catalogued Dan Kiley Collection available to us.

Many individuals graciously provided personal perspectives and helped to define the symposium's goals and objectives. Here we are most grateful to A.E. Bye, Garrett Eckbo, Paul Friedberg, Richard Haag, Lawrence Halprin, Gary Hilderbrand, Carol Johnson, Dan Kiley, Cornelia Oberlander, Beth Meyer, John Simonds, and Marc Treib for their generosity of time and thoughtful insights. The Graham Foundation for Advanced Studies in the Fine Arts and the National Park Service, Historic Preservation Services Programs, also provided partial support.

In making this publication a reality, Jane Brown Gillette and Sarah Vance at Spacemaker Press have been inspiration shepherds. We are most grateful for Jane's assistance, which began as a general editor in 1997 when she was still working at *Landscape Architecture* magazine.

Thanks to National Park Service colleagues Kay D. Weeks and Bryan Green, who lent editorial support, and to deTeel Patterson Tiller, Sharon C. Park, and Antoinette Lee, who also supported this endeavor.

Finally, thanks to Peter Walker for suggesting the Spacemaker Press Landmark Series as an appropriate vehicle to present this diverse collection of papers. We hope that this is just the beginning of an expanded conversation between those who design and those who preserve.—*Charles A. Birnbaum*

Table of Contents

Preface:
Sharp Angles or Curves?
You Decide

Charles A. Birnbaum

As I write this introduction and revisit the papers from the Preserving Modern Landscape Architecture conference held at Wave Hill in November 1995, I ask a simple question: Why is it that the profession has to be hit over the head with the twenty-pound *Architecture and Urbanism Between the Second World War and the Bicentennial* by Robert A.M. Stern and others before we'll even consider developing an equally in-depth contextual statement for modern American landscape architecture? Without such a manifesto the importance of modernist landscapes will remain invisible to all but a few. Where are the vehicles that will help the public share our vision? As we consider these questions, the following three events occur simultaneously:

■   A group of tree-lovers in Camden, Maine, is opposing a restoration plan for Fletcher Steele's Garden Amphitheater, designed in 1929. Steele's revolutionary application of a bent axis may be its first application in a public modernist garden in America. If the context for this work and others of the period is established, then the importance of this masterwork will be indisputable.

■   *Numbers 1964* by Jasper Johns, which hangs at Lincoln Center's New York State Theater, was almost sold for $15 million. *New York Times* reporter Roberta Smith refers to the Johns painting as "a living work of art" (1/25/99). In the articles that follow, no mention is made of the courtyard design by landscape architect Daniel Urban Kiley, and there is no discussion of its future treatment and management.

■   The outlook for the Thomas Church residence in San Francisco is, at best, uncertain. Ironic, considering that a lesser-known Church design for the Fay-Berrigan residence (1957-1958) has been saved in the past year. Where is the concerned constituency today, and why are they slow to rally around preserving the designer's own home?

Things may not really be this bleak. For example, consider the response by universities, professional organizations, and related arts facilities. In the three years since the Wave Hill conference was held, there has been an increased professional discourse on the topic. This response can be seen in the form of symposia and related exhibitions. In two cases there are even plans to publish the proceedings. In all cases these papers have been broad in both subject and geography—a testimony to the diversity of projects, to the designers who created them, and to the critics who wrote about them. The four symposia that followed Wave Hill include:

■   Landscape Architecture: Recovery Into Prosperity, 1940-1960, a two-day symposium cosponsored by the College of Environmental Design, University of California at Berkeley, and the Berkeley Art Museum/Pacific Film Archives, explored the international social, political, and artistic forces that influenced the profession (February 1997);

■   Dan Kiley, Landscape Architect—the First Two Decades, a one-day symposium and month-long exhibition at Harvard University's Graduate School of Design organized by Joseph Disponzio, highlighted Kiley's least-known work and re-examined some of his best-known designs (November 1997);

■   Thomas Church: The Gardens and the Gardeners, a symposium sponsored by the Department of Landscape Architecture and Environmental Planning at Berkeley and organized by Marc Treib, concerned the design, care, and preservation of the landscapes of Thomas Church (February 1998); and

■   J.B. Jackson and American Landscape, organized by the School of Architecture and Planning at the University of New Mexico, Albuquerque, was an interdisciplinary assessment of the future of cultural landscape studies in addition to evaluations of Jackson's ideas and impact (October 1998).

Abroad, our knowledge base also increases. DOCOMO, the international working party for documentation and conservation of buildings, sites, and neighborhoods of the modern movement, included presentations on modern gardens at their fourth international conference in Bratislava, Slovakia, in September 1996, on Universality and Heterogeneity. Landscape and Garden in Britain: 1930-2000, sponsored by the Garden History Society and the Twentieth Century Society, the first-ever conference on modern landscape architecture in Britain, drew more than 250 participants in Kew Gardens. This March 1998 symposium pursued a multidisciplinary approach to landscape architecture, encompassing rural and urban planning as well as garden design. As a result of the symposium, a national study is currently being undertaken by English Heritage to "improve the protection of modern landscapes."

Thanks to these professional achievements, significant works of landscape architecture may now have a better chance of survival. As a result, an assumption can be made that there is an ever-increasing awareness of modern landscape architecture at a variety of professional levels. Today this growing constituency includes practicing landscape architects, architects, and landscape, architectural, and social historians—many of whom recognize the benefits of the preservation and/or documentation of these nationally significant works. Now that more has been done to develop an expanded professional forum, what about the general public? Consider these recent developments:

■   Central Park's Adventure Playground at 67th Street has been restored and upgraded to meet contemporary safety requirements; a new design and rehabilitation scheme has been adopted for the playground at P.S. 166 on West 89th Street in New York City; the Lake Anne Village Center has been rehabilitated and its focal concrete fountain restored in Reston, Virginia; and attempts are being made to preserve Gas Works Park in Seattle, Washington. In each of these cases the original designer, including architect Richard Dattner, landscape architect M. Paul Friedberg, village designer James Rossant, and landscape architect Richard Haag, were actively consulted and participated in dialogues with the present-day professionals, the stewards of the resource, and the interested communities. Moreover, in all of these cases affiliated "friends" groups played an active role in the process and created the impetus for considering these projects as rehabilitation projects. Ultimately, more than just new design, they were historic preservation endeavors.

Lyndhurst, Tarrytown, New York

The 1960s version of Copley Square, Boston, Massachusetts, Sasaki, Dawson, and DeMay Associates

How can these success stories be better understood and shared with a broader public? How can we take the steps to nurture a greater public interest in the future of our designed landscapes? Why does the public so often allow the demolition or complete overhaul of modernist works? Research findings about public tastes and perceptions published in Vitaly Komar and Aleksandr Melamid's *Painting by Numbers* (1997) provide valuable clues.

Russian immigrant artists Komar and Melamid, assisted by a professional polling firm, conducted a survey of what Americans, regardless of class, race, or gender, really want in art. This scientific poll surveyed 1,001 American adults. Questions included: What is beauty? Who defines it? And why is high art so remote from most people? Using the survey results, Komar and Melamid painted the works that were deemed "America's Most Wanted" and "America's Most Unwanted." The conclusion about aesthetic attributes in painting can also apply to works of landscape architecture:

Art should be relaxing to look at	66% agree	15% disagree
Realistic or different-looking?	44% realistic	25% different
Sharp angles or curves?	22% sharp angles	61% soft curves
Colors blended or separate?	45% colors blended	20% separate
Favorite color	24% blue	15% green

Apply these "values" to two significant American landscapes. The first is a pastoral view over the deer park at Lyndhurst, a National Trust property in Tarrytown, New York, laid out in the mid-nineteenth century, while the second is an aerial view of the 1960s Sasaki, Dawson and DeMay Associates design for Boston's Copley Square. A quick look at these images readily reveals that those landscapes of the historic Hudson River Valley and the works of pioneering landscape architects Frederick Law Olmsted, Sr., and Jens Jensen possess the same characteristics that appear in art that is "most wanted" in this country. Conversely, the aerial photograph of Copley Square, like Lawrence Halprin's design for San Francisco's Embarcadero Center, Richard Serra's *Tilted Arc* in New York City, and Dan Kiley's design for the Burr sculpture court in Hartford all reveal the same commonalities. They each possess many of the same characteristics that appear in the "most unwanted" painting—thus presenting to the visitor a monochromatic, architectonic scene deemed unfamiliar and even unnerving. It is no surprise that the "shelf life" of each of these projects has been less than twenty years and that they have often become highly controversial.

In an article that appeared the week after the Wave Hill conference in *The New York Times,* columnist Anne Raver noted that "these invisible landscapes are being taken up by a growing number of landscape architects around the country, who are organizing to protect their work, both as works of art and as vessels of cultural history."

Perhaps Raver's statement (paraphrasing *Invisible Gardens* by Peter Walker and Melanie Simo) holds the key to this situation. The future of this irreplaceable legacy lies in the hands of the professional community of landscape architects, who are increasingly doing a better job of educating themselves and must now communicate with the public about the significance and uniqueness of these distinctive places.

It seems appropriate to end with a reminder of the current Lincoln Center controversy—especially since a number of the papers that follow celebrate Dan Kiley's scheme at the Lincoln Center project. The Jasper Johns saga captured the attention of New York and national media. Following its resolution, the president of the authority stated in the press that "they planned to raise money to improve the buildings and were confident that they could do it without selling assets." Yet unresolved is the fate of the Dan Kiley-designed campus that supports the building and collections. Invisible still?

Charles A. Birnbaum, FASLA
Coordinator, Historic Landscape Initiative
National Park Service, Heritage Preservation Services
Washington DC

May 1999

Preserving Contemporary Landscape Architecture: Is Nothing Permanent But Change Itself?

Charles A. Birnbaum

"We live in a world whose advances are based on the continuous expansion of the use of the scientific method, beyond those fields called exact, to such as esthetics and sociology. The scientific method is one which takes nothing for granted, accepts no precedents without examination, and recognizes a dynamic world in which nothing is permanent but change itself."

Garrett Eckbo, *Landscape for Living* (1950)

When we think of the treatment of historic designed landscapes we often think about the preservation of the works of Frederick Law Olmsted, Sr., Jens Jensen, or Beatrix Farrand—to name three well-known pioneers of the profession. When we consider the contributions of contemporary visionaries such as Lawrence Halprin, Dan Kiley, James Rose, or Hideo Sasaki, we don't often think of their landscapes as historic resources requiring special protection. Well, think again.

It was not too long ago that the first printing of Norman T. Newton's *Design on the Land* (1971) included a perspective rendering of the "outstanding design" for Copley Square by Sasaki, Dawson, and DeMay Associates (1966) with the caption, "the famous Copley Square redesigned at last."[1] It is ironic that while Newton's book can still be found on bookstore shelves, the redesigned Copley Square has since seen another design competition (1983) and a complete reconstruction (1989).

A.E. Bye, FASLA, recalls a recent conversation with Lawrence Halprin, FASLA: "Larry stated that we spend thirty to forty years trying to get our projects built and then the next ten to twenty years trying to make sure that they don't get knocked down."[2] In a telephone conversation with Halprin his frustrations are immediately apparent: "If a painting or sculpture is purchased, it is safe to assume that it will be respected. A house or landscape, however, may be brought down."[3]

Over the past few years a substantial number of landscapes from the recent past have been put at risk or altered substantially. These range from residential designs by Bye (Gainesway Farms in Lexington, Kentucky), Thomas Church (the Thomas Church residence in San Francisco, California), and Jane Platt (the Jane Platt garden in Portland); streetscapes, squares, and plazas by Dan Kiley (Independence Mall in Philadelphia and Burr Sculpture Court in Hartford) or Lawrence Halprin (Nicollet Mall in Minneapolis and the Embarcadero Fountain in San Francisco); nearly all of the shopping-center designs by Louise Shellhorn (Bullock Wilshire in Pasadena and Sherman Oaks in the San Fernando Valley); parks by Richard Haag and Jones & Jones (Occidental Park in Seattle) and Kiley (Jefferson National Expansion Memorial/Gateway Arch Memorial Landscape in St. Louis); and campus plans by Kiley (Concordia Junior College in Fort Wayne, Indiana, and the United States Air Force Academy at Colorado Springs); zoos by Clarke & Rapuano (at Central Park in New York City) and William C. Pauley (Grant Park Zoo in Atlanta); and exposition grounds by Clarke & Rapuano (New York World's Fair, now Flushing Meadows Corona Park) and Haag (1962 Seattle World's Fair, now Seattle Center).

One central issue in preserving built landscapes of the recent past is that of integrity, which is defined by the National Register of Historic Places as "the authenticity of a property's historic identity, evidenced by the survival of physical characteristics that existed during the property's historic period."[4] Thus, if features critical to the overall significance of the design are removed or altered, the integrity of the design will most likely be compromised. For example, consider the removal of native bank plantings and their replacement with a mown lawn at Colby College, Waterville, Maine (design by Carol Johnson Associates); the elimination of a bosque composed of symmetrical groupings of London plane trees and their replacement with solitary Bradford pear trees at Lincoln Center in New York City (Kiley); the elimination of well-established foundation plantings to accommodate new above-ground ventilation ducts at Robson Square in Vancouver, British Columbia (Cornelia Oberlander); unresolved replacement challenges posed by the death of two sentinel California live oaks at the Dewey Donnell Ranch in Sonoma (Thomas Church); and the recent replacement of a fountain designed by Halprin for the 1962 Seattle World's Fair with a work of contemporary sculpture.

Probably the greatest loss occurs with the redesign and/or enclosure of outdoor regional shopping centers and their associated landscaped spaces—an action that eradicates an important chapter in the profession's evolution from the mid-1950s to the late 1960s. Although not outright demolition, another unfortunate scenario in landscape projects of this era has been the "upgrading" of site-specific character-defining pavements, lights, and streetscape furnishings that are now difficult to maintain or are perceived as out of fashion. In the case of the recently altered Nicollet Mall, Lance Neckar, ASLA, points out that "the mall was an experiment—designed using new, untested materials that were not durable or appropriate to Minnesota. It became costly to maintain over the long term. (For example, the maintenance of the lights alone ran $100,000 annually.) As a formal idea we regret its passing, yet the local group was adamant that it had to change."[5]

Given a variety of limitations and both physical and natural pressures, what are the possibilities for the documentation, evaluation, and preservation of this recent, yet important legacy? We suggest the following:

1. Pursue nominations to the National Register for recent landscape architecture.
According to *National Register Bulletin 22: Guidelines for Evaluating and Nominating Properties That Have Achieved Significance Within the Last Fifty Years*, "As a general rule, properties that have achieved significance within the last fifty years are not eligible for National Register listing because the Register is intrinsically a compilation of the nation's historic resources that are worthy of preservation. The National Register does not include properties solely for their contemporary impact and visibility, and it rarely is possible to evaluate historical impact, role, or relative value immediately after an event occurs or a building is constructed. The passage of time is necessary in order to apply the adjective 'historic' and to ensure adequate perspective."[6]

Nevertheless, justification for significance has been achieved for a number of modern architectural examples: In fact, there are nearly one thousand buildings on the National Register that fit this category. One such example is the Whitney Museum of American Art, New York, constructed between 1963 and 1966. The nomination states that the Whitney "is of exceptional significance as the work of an internationally acclaimed master, Marcel Breuer, whose work had a profound influence on the course of American architecture, and as a representative of the Expressionist movement in modern American architecture during the 1950s and 1960s."[7] Within this established framework works of modern landscape architecture could be nominated with sufficient context.

Nicollet Mall, Minneapolis, Minnesota, Lawrence Halprin, 1967

Independence Mall, Philadelphia, Pennsylvania, Dan Kiley, 1963

2. Establish a larger context for contemporary landscape architecture.

In the past few years there has been a dramatic increase in scholarly works with a focus on recent landscape architectural history. Examples include *Richard Haag: Bloedel Reserve and Gas Works Park*, edited by William Saunders (1998); Marc Treib and Dorothee Imbert's *Garrett Eckbo: Modern Landscapes for Living* (1997); Peter Walker and Melanie Simo's *Invisible Gardens: The Search for Modernism in the American Landscape* (1994); Treib's *Modern Landscape Architecture: A Critical Review* (1993), Imbert's *The Modernist Garden in France* (1993); Felice Frankel and Jory Johnson's *Modern Landscape Architecture: Redefining the Garden* (1991) with many more works on the immediate horizon. Other invaluable forms of contextual history are contained in thematic issues of *Process Architecture*—each written by the designer. Issues have already considered the works of Garrett Eckbo, M. Paul Friedberg, Dan Kiley, The SWA Group, Peter Walker, and Robert Zion.

Another rich source of historical context can be found in oral histories with significant designers. For example, the Hubbard Educational Trust over the past few years has funded oral histories of Gilmore Clarke, Garrett Eckbo, Norman Newton, Arthur A. Shurcliffe, and Charles Eliot II; Pennsylvania State University has videotaped interviews with several John R. Bracken fellows and lecturers including Bye, Ian McHarg, Roberto Burle Marx, Roderick Nash, Sir Geoffrey Jellicoe, and John Simonds; and the University of California Regional Oral History Office, Bancroft Library, has undertaken oral histories of such California figures as Thomas Church.

3. Document threatened work.

Masterworks in particular should be documented, especially if they are threatened with change. This would have been extremely useful for Nicollet Mall, especially since no as-built plans are known to exist. Another example that is at current risk is Gainesway Farms in Lexington, Kentucky. Considered by many to be one of Bye's most significant works (executed 1974-1982), it has recently been sold. Upon hearing rumors of redesign to include new fences and alterations to character-defining topography and plantings, Bye made a site visit to meet with the new owners. According to Bye, "they did not have a meeting of the minds." Like many Bye designs there are no project drawings generated by his office other than those produced for later publications.

Although the Historic American Building Survey (HABS) contains no documentation of modern works other than what is contained in associated project photography, this is about to change. HABS is negotiating with the American Institute of Architects (AIA), which has established a HABS advisory board. Says Paul Dolinsky, HABS chief, "When a building receives a twenty-five-year award from the AIA, the original architects' drawings would be submitted to HABS as part of this recognition, and the as-builts would become a part of the HABS collection."[8]

Therefore, a precedent exists for works of landscape architecture to be prepared for permanent accession into the Library of Congress collections.

4. Avoid cultural amnesia: Consult with the original designer when possible.

Carol Johnson, FASLA, points out that a continuum of design can often provide many advantages. She suggests that the original landscape architect may have "an understanding of what people were like then and now, coupled with a knowledge of the history of the landscape both in detail and how it evolved."[9] For example, Halprin has recently been called back to the Lovejoy Fountain in Portland, Oregon, to consult on issues of maintenance, lighting, and the perimeter trees, which have matured to such a degree "that views into this much beloved space are no longer possible."[10] With regard to revisiting his design Halprin queries, "Where does history stop, and how far back do you go?" He also recognizes that "sometimes things need to be changed, and a new society or series of events warrant new design."[11] This philosophical framework has had an immediate impact on establishing the design intent for the Lovejoy Fountain rehabilitation.

5. Educate owners and public stewards.

At all levels of the profession we should strive to educate public municipalities and private owners about the significance of these properties. This is precisely what Dean Cardesis, ASLA, University of Massachusetts at Amherst, and others are undertaking for the James Rose house, as well as for his extant legacy of residential designs. Today Rose's house in Ridgewood, New Jersey, is managed and owned by a not-for-profit, The James Rose Center for Landscape Architectural Research and Design. The challenge for this group is to arrest the further deterioration of a property that evolved in accordance with Rose's own design philosophies between 1953 and 1980 and deteriorated after Rose's death. The fruits of these labors have already been evidenced through a consortium of sponsors that include the Garden Conservancy, academic institutions, local sponsors, and assistance from other owners of James Rose landscapes—the latter now having a greater interest in their own landscapes. (For more about The James Rose Center, see Dean Cardesis's article on Page 24.)

6. Establish creative partnerships.

Antonia Adezio, executive director of the Garden Conservancy, suggests that "a lot of what we do is association."[12] Formed in 1989, the Conservancy has assisted a number of owners and interested community groups. Part of its mission is to "preserve fine gardens beyond the mortality of their creators and their ephemeral natures, to fortify the gardener's artistic vision so that it may be shared with generations of gardeners yet to come."[13]

One recent example of the Conservancy's efforts has been its involvement with Jane Platt's garden in Portland, Oregon. Platt's garden has been well-known in horticultural circles for many years, but the future of this garden following her death in 1992 had been uncertain. The Conservancy has developed a management plan and enlisted the support of the local garden club, which has assisted in the maintenance of what Adezio refers to as a "very personal garden."[14] (John Fitzpatrick tells more about the Garden Conservancy on Page 78.)

7. Ensure proper homes for archives.

Finding a home for landscape architects' archives can be as challenging as convincing practitioners to donate their collections to an institution. The situation over the past few years has improved considerably, with many institutions ready and willing to accept collections that include contemporary works. The University of Pennsylvania, for example, recently accepted the collections of Halprin, George E. Patton, and Philip N. Winslow, while the Special Collections Library of the Harvard Graduate School of Design has acquired a large portion of Kiley's office collection and the University of California at Berkeley has acquired the Thomas Church archives.

8. Utilize current standards and guidelines when embarking on project work.

The National Park Service provides technical assistance for registering, nominating, analyzing, treating, and managing historic landscapes. Sympathetic applications of these tools and methodologies should be considered and tailored to these unique resources.[15]

9. Formulate a national strategy.

The ASLA and/or the Landscape Architecture Foundation should develop a strategy to safeguard this legacy through a special committee of recognized landscape historians and scholars. The committee should strive to evaluate and recognize those significant landscapes that are threatened with change or eradication. It could utilize criteria modeled after such programs as the NPS Landmarks at Risk program. Maintaining an arm of the ASLA to honor the contemporary masterworks that have stood the test of time is essential if we are to maintain an honest and complete record, provide a tool to enlighten ourselves and the general public, and ultimately ensure their survival.

As architectural historian Richard Longstreth has recently stated, "If we continue to disregard so much that is all around us, we may waste far more than preserve and bestow upon future generations the difficult task of deciphering the carcass."[16] We must be committed to these landscapes that are often a part of our everyday lives, even those that we take for granted. If we allow these losses and modifications to continue—unmonitored by the profession and allied communities—we run the risk of erasing a significant chapter of landscape history.

Robson Square, Vancouver, British Columbia, Arthur Erickson Architects, Cornelia Oberlander, and Raoul Robillard

James Rose Center, Ridgewood, New Jersey

1 Norman T. Newton, *Design on the Land: The Development of Landscape Architecture* (Cambridge: Harvard University Press, 1971), 652.

2 A.E. Bye, telephone conversation with the author, April 1995.

3 Lawrence Halprin, telephone conversations with the author, March and April 1995.

4 *National Register Bulletin 16A: How to Complete the National Register Form* (Washington, D.C.: U.S. Department of the Interior, National Park Service, Interagency Resources Division, 1991).

5 Lance Neckar, telephone conversation with the author, Spring 1995.

6 *National Register Bulletin 22: Guidelines for Evaluating and Nominating Properties That Have Achieved Significance Within the Last Fifty Years* (Washington, D.C.: U.S. Department of the Interior, National Park Service, Interagency Resources Division, rev. ed., 1996), 1.

7 See the detailed nomination for the Whitney Museum contained in the National Register Files, Washington, D.C. This listing is included in a recent ninety-two-page printout of "buildings with less than fifty years of significance" from the National Register.

8 Paul Dolinsky, telephone conversation with the author, April 1995.

9 Carol Johnson, telephone conversation with the author, April 1995.

10 Lawrence Halprin, telephone conversation with the author, April 1995.

11 Ibid.

12 Antonia Adezio, telephone conversation with the author, April 1995.

13 Ibid.

14 Ibid.

15 The National Park Service's Historic Landscape Initiative provides technical assistance and training opportunities. Visit their website at www2.nps.cr.gov/hli

16 Richard Longstreth, "The Significance of the Recent Past," *APT Bulletin* (1991), 12-24.

Preserving the Recent Design Past

Peter E. Walker

The Miller Garden, Columbus, Indiana, Dan Kiley

First, I want to emphasize that I am not a trained historian or preservationist. My entry into twentieth-century history has been a search for some kind of understanding of my own time and work, as a practitioner. Our book, *Invisible Gardens* (1994), was a psychological or family analysis that I ventured into with art historian Melanie Simo as my guide. It has been a fascinating experience. I am, however, a lifelong garden enthusiast as well as a designer. I hope you will take what I have to say in this light.

Within contemporary American culture it is extremely unlikely that a work of landscape architecture can achieve the accepted status of a work of art. That is not to say that I don't view landscape architecture as basically an art form rather than a part of the science of ecology, no matter how useful that point of view has been for landscape architects over the last twenty years. But it is unlikely that a garden can be accepted as a work of art for many reasons, including the following:

First, the design profession is small and, to a large degree, unknown. It does not have a large following or patronage, it has little criticism or press, and there are almost no connoisseurs. As Dan Kiley has said, most people who are interested in gardens know very little about them, including designers. Most designers, therefore, only occasionally have the opportunity of a real patronage situation.

Second, our culture is becoming increasingly commercial, and it depends more and more on media rather than physical travel for cultural access. This means that fewer people see gardens in person, and, as John Dixon Hunt has pointed out, landscape is essentially an art of milieu. An image rarely conveys the essence of this art form. Geographic diversity adds to the difficulty of seeing actual gardens, and the specifics of site and program allow little seriality of project, making the body of work of one designer less likely to attract media attention.

Third, landscape is often seen as a social art, and our public social life during the modern era has been in a state of constant and often violent change, with each change of direction denying the validity of each preceding direction.

Fourth, it is axiomatic that a garden must be grown over time rather than constructed in a moment like architecture. It must then also be maintained throughout its life. The rate of change makes both continuity of patronage or stewardship over time less likely. It is rare that the patronage impulse withstands the changing ownerships, administrations, and budget attitudes throughout these years of growth.

Fifth, private grounds, domestic or corporate, often go through years, perhaps decades, of private ownership prior to becoming limitedly or generally public. These years may make them culturally invisible to the generation for which they are made and to those who might be expected to love and care about them or appreciate their iconic or artistic value.

Sixth, the rapid changes in popular taste—or perceived functional need—make major reconstruction or removal a more or less constant threat.

Seventh, rapid cultural change tends to shorten institutional memory, and the point of a design may be lost to its owners or caretakers. And to the next generation of designers. Even among academically trained designers history has typically been the weakest part of their education. Only a few schools have professional historians.

For these reasons I would argue that the length of time to culturally qualify a garden, compared to, say, a work of architecture, puts at unfair disadvantage a work of landscape art.

Many of these difficulties and ambiguities are actually embedded in the cultural phenomenon we term modernism, and yet, with all of these difficulties, there are still a few rare projects that have achieved high cultural status. What are the qualities of these projects that have made them exemplars, and how did these qualities come into being? Also, what is their current condition, and what are their future prospects, absent new approaches and attitudes within our culture?

The first really great modern garden I ever saw was Dan Kiley's garden for Irwin Miller. I first went to Columbus, Indiana, in 1956 with Dan while I was a graduate student at the University of Illinois in Champaign-Urbana. We drove down over the brick highways of southern Illinois and Indiana and spent the day there during the initial construction phase of the garden. The staggered hedges, the outdoor pool room, the point grids, and crossaxial locust allée were all roughly in place. To be frank, although I found it interesting at the time, I had no notion that I was viewing what is perhaps the most important modern American garden.

Years later, in 1978, the Harvard landscape department commissioned a series of photographs by Alan Ward of the Miller Garden and other Kiley gardens for an exhibit at the Harvard Graduate School of Design. By the late 1970s the garden had matured. Planting and technical difficulties had been resolved, and the full impact of Kiley's concept could be seen. The maintenance has always been impeccable and loving. This is a masterwork—a product of a great design and a continuously engaged patron of taste.

They tell a story (I'm not sure if it's true) about Kevin Roche's complaining to Eero Saarinen about the twin beech trees due west of the living room of the house. Saarinen was supposed to have replied, "Let's just this one time let [Kiley] do what he wants!" It is ironic that the garden, even though rarely seen by practitioners (it was only published incognito early in its existence), has been one of the most influential and timeless of modern American gardens while the house has receded into relative obscurity.

More recently, as Kiley has at last become well known, the Miller Garden is beginning to receive the analysis and critical attention it deserves. The modernism it expresses clearly extends from architectural spatial thought rather than from modern painting, separating Kiley from most of his contemporaries. The interlocking grids are a fusion of LeNotre's spatial power and Meisian industrial spatial-structural thinking. It is the most clear of all of Kiley's "modern" architectural designs—complex and witty, but made in a direct and simple way. Grading, planting, and paving combine to offer both surprise and calm.

Although Irwin Miller and his son, Will Miller, remain two of the most important patrons of our time, no one really knows the fate of the garden and what its public or professional availability may be. It is perhaps interesting to compare the Miller Garden to the public park that Kiley designed in 1988 in Tampa, Florida, with the architect Harry Wolf. Here, a much more complex and layered garden with exquisitely detailed water elements is being maintained indifferently as a public park by the local parks department. Although installed much later than the Miller Garden, it is already in serious decline.

One of the most frequently photographed gardens of our time is Thomas Church's Donnell Garden, in Sonoma, California. The pool, terrace, and lanais were designed and installed in 1947-1948, and the house and lower garden were built a few years later. Both Lawrence Halprin and George Rockrise played associate roles in the design. The pool sculpture by Adeline Kent extends the Jean Arp-like forms into the vertical dimension.

This garden is not typical of Church's earlier work, which often showed interesting signs of transition from earlier formal vocabularies. This was one of the first complete examples of Church's fusion of the carpenter constructivism—influenced by his long association with the architect William Wurster—and surrealism, perhaps showing the influence of his interest in and knowledge of Alvar Aalto's Finnish architecture and gardens as well as his contact with modern European art.

With his usual fine instinct for siting, Church placed the terrace at the edge of a bluff overlooking the salt marshes at the north end of San Francisco Bay. But many aspects of this garden are unique: among them, an idealized purity of expression, the indoor-outdoor fusion of architecture and garden, and the elegant manner in which its spatiality lends itself to a series of memorable images representing Church's ideal of casual, yet refined California leisure and freedom. The family has kept the garden in wonderful condition over the years. It is the best-maintained of all of Church's important gardens. Many of his others have been lost.

I first visited CIGNA (then called Connecticut General Insurance Company) in the suburbs of Hartford, Connecticut, in 1959, when it was under construction. I was then working with Bruce Graham of Skidmore, Owings & Merrill (SOM) on a new headquarters for the Upjohn Company in Kalamazoo, Michigan. Graham took me there to meet Gordon Bunschaft, CIGNA's architect, to see the buildings and particularly to inspect the site development, courtyards, and terraces designed by Isamu Noguchi with the assistance of Joanna Diman, a landscape architect with SOM. Even before its completion the word was out through the SOM network that a remarkable project was under way and that the collaboration of Bunschaft and Noguchi was again producing a modern icon.

I remember particularly the elegant simplicity of the entry drives, the long, low-lying siting of the buildings, and the gently rolling yet taut shaping of the small lake and meadow. But what impressed me most were the surreal courtyard gardens and the main terrace adjacent to the cafeteria that overlooked the pond. In both the entry drives and the terrace the materials (stone, gravel, ground covers, and trees) seemed effortless and right. The carved stone fountains and occasional bench were completely integrated within the curved and straight lines of the various compositions. The effect was magical and yet very economical. Here, textures of ground covers, grass, gravels, and flagstones, together with

Courtyards, CIGNA Headquarters, Hartford, Connecticut, Isamu Noguchi

the shadows cast from the building and the trees, created visual compositions of remarkable originality and great beauty.

During the next ten or fifteen years the gardens matured and softened, and they, like the building, received loving maintenance. When I took my first Harvard class to see them in 1976, company representatives showed us the gardens with great pride. We were given printed histories, and the gardens were described in some detail.

On our visits over the next dozen years or so several things began to happen. The gardens began to change. Unintended seasonal flowers were added to beds that had none before. The pools were drained, and the gorgeous tile linings were removed and not replaced. Steps were replaced by ramps covered with Astroturf to provide handicapped access, and the institutional memory began to fail. The handouts disappeared, and although the maintenance continued to be excellent, it often altered—rather than continued—the design intent. I found myself explaining the meaning and importance of the gardens to the company employees. The sense of stewardship that had developed and sustained this great design faltered, then dulled, and by 1990 finally failed.

The building and the overall site have never looked better. New additions have been done with great care, and a large, new, but inferior building has been placed out of sight of the original complex. But the *piece de resistance*, the visual heart of the icon, the courtyards and terrace are disintegrating from lack of memory. They could easily and quite inexpensively be restored. But the ideas have deteriorated. Why can't something be done to repair this truly great work of modernism?

The Pepsico World Headquarters gardens at Purchase, New York, were laid out by landscape architect Edward Durrell Stone, Jr., working with his father, the architect Edward Durrell Stone. The original site plan was one of the most interesting and ingenious of the postwar corporate palaces in that it separated the surface parking lots from the building and its surrounding gardens by deep bands of existing woods. One would arrive, park, and then in all seasons walk on gently curving wooded paths across lawns dotted with sculpture, only then to arrive at and enter the building proper. Employees and visitors experienced the landscape on each and every visit. VIPs entered through a smaller automobile court. A lovely tree-shaded terrace extended the cafeteria out to grand, long views of the lake and the more monumental sculpture.

For Donald Kendall, then CEO of Pepsico and the major collector of the sculpture, this was a very good start but not a complete realization of his vision for the garden. He next hired Russell Page, the famous English landscape gardener, to further develop and refine the gardens. This refinement went on until Page's death in 1985 and continues still, under the direction of Page's assistant. Page added to Stone's original armature ingenious plantings that in texture, color, and form make the garden a rich delight even without the extensive collection of art, which includes a great Noguchi stone, a fine Calder stabile, the Oldenburg trowel, a wonderful Rickey, and many, many others. Often the color or form of the sculpture is contrasted or extended in the remarkable choice and placement of plants. Kendall, now retired, is still active in the on-going growth of the garden and can often be seen strolling the grounds or talking to visitors.

Because Pepsico is a public company and therefore presumed to be a stable institution, one can hope for the longevity of the garden after Kendall's death. But one has only to look at the Upjohn headquarters in Kalamazoo, Michigan, to see that no matter the size or quality of the gardens, neither they nor institutional memory will necessarily last forever.

Lawrence Halprin's Lovejoy Fountain in Portland, Oregon, is an exquisitely personal artistic statement—and one of the most important and beautiful public places built since World War II. It is a work from 1961, perhaps the Halprin office's most productive and busy time. And yet, in my judgment, it stands above all of their other important work of that period. Along with Halprin, Satora Nashita and Charles Moore are generally credited with the design. Moore designed the complex and mysterious arbor at the top of the fountain and may have critically assisted the entirety of the project. The fountain concept comes from Halprin's extensive hiking trips into, and hundreds of drawings of, the Sierra Nevada Mountains. It is conceived as a mountain stream, coursing through a vertical opening, twisting as it falls to a boiling froth, then crashing down to spread out over a great smooth, flat, and finally quiet pool. Except for the wooden arbor it is made entirely of poured concrete expressed in a constantly changing series of vertical and horizontal slabs, reminiscent of the violent German Expressionist paintings and sculptures from between the wars. Ada Louise Huxtable has called it the greatest public fountain since those of the Baroque masters.

The fountain's most problematic quality is that it is made entirely of poured reinforced concrete, a material dear to modernists but one that has been proven to wear rather poorly—even in the mild climate of Portland.

These projects are but a few of the thousands of gardens installed over the last sixty years or so. From my own experience I could have mentioned at least several hundred. Just think of the work of Roberto Burle Marx, Luis Barragan, Garrett Eckbo, Robert Royston, Richard Haag, or Hideo Sasaki. And what of the Europeans and the Japanese of this period? How many gardens do we not even know? How many have been destroyed or allowed to disintegrate? Many were, and some still are, alive and beautiful. A few are culturally important and wonderful. They represent for me some of our culture's best impulses.

Peter Walker, FASLA, is a landscape architect with Peter Walker and Partners, Berkeley, California, and editor in chief of Land Forum.

Lovejoy Plaza, Portland, Oregon, Lawrence Halprin

Donnell Garden, Sonoma, California, Thomas Church and his associates, 1948-1951

Post World-War II Landscape Architecture in the United States
Elizabeth K. Meyer

1940s

1945
Point State Park, GWSM
1947
Levittown, New York
Jefferson National
    Expansion Memorial
    competition, Dan Kiley
1949
Donnell Garden,
    Thomas Church

Donnell Garden

Jefferson National Expansion Memorial

1950s

1950
Ellen Shipman dies
Greendale Extension
    Elbert Peets
1951
Jens Jensen dies.
Bloedel Reserve, Thomas
    Church and, later,
    Richard Haag
1950
Levittown, Pennsylvania
Palisades Interstate
    Parkway, New Jersey
    section, Clarke and
    Rapuano
1952
Naumkeag Rose Garden,
    Fletcher Steele

1954
Rose residence and
    garden, James Rose
1955
Levittown, New Jersey
Naumkeag Chinese Garden
    wall, Fletcher Steele
Miller Garden, Dan Kiley
Museum of Modern Art
    Sculpture Garden,
    Philip Johnson
Standard Oil Rod and Gun
    Club, EDAW, Inc.
George Washington
    Memorial Parkway,
    Clarke and Howland

1957
Frederick Law Olmsted, Jr.,
dies.
CIGNA, SOM and Isamu
    Noguchi
Foothill College,
    Upjohn Corporation
    Headquarters, Sasaki
    Walker Associates
1958
Dulles Airport, Rockefeller
    University, Dan Kiley
1959
Alcoa Forecast Garden,
    Garrett Eckbo
United States Air Force
    Academy, Dan Kiley
Mellon Square, Simonds
    and Simonds
Beatrix Ferrand dies.
Carol R. Johnson opens
office.

12

1960s

1960
Stanford University Plaza,
    Thomas Church
Lincoln Center, Dan Kiley
1961
Columbia, Maryland
MacIntyre Garden, Portland
    Open Space Sequence,
    Lawrence Halprin
1962
Sea Pines Plantation, Hilton
Head, Sasaki Walker
    Associates
Oakland Museum,
    Dan Kiley
1963
Plan for the Valleys,
    McHarg, Wallace,
    Roberts, Todd
Reston, Virginia
Independence Mall,
    Dan Kiley

1964
John Deere Headquarters,
    Sasaki Walker
    Associates
1965
Ghirardelli Square,
    Lawrence Halprin
Riis Park, Paul Friedberg
Constitution Plaza, Sasaki
    Walker Associates
1966
Copley Square, Sasaki
    Dawson, and Demay
    Associates
1967
Soros Garden, A.E. Bye
Paley Park, Zion and Breen
Nicollet Mall, and Sea
    Ranch, Lawrence Halprin
1968
Elbert Peets dies.
Sidney Walton Park,
    Sasaki Walker
    Associates

Lincoln Center

Portland Open Space Sequence

Sea Pines Plantation

Independence Mall

Naumkeag Rose Garden

James Rose residence

Bloedel Reserve

Miller Garden

CIGNA

Foothill College

Upjohn Corporation

United States Air Force Academy

Dulles Airport

John Deere Headquarters

Ghirardelli Square

Constitution Plaza

Copley Square

Soros Garden

Nicollet Mall

Sea Ranch

Sydney Walton Park

Preservation in the Age of Ecology: Post-World War II Built Landscapes

Elizabeth K. Meyer

What images, individuals, and ideas are conjured up when we think about the post-World War II American landscape? Houses, housing, roads, neighborhoods, shopping malls, suburbs, new towns, campuses, both academic and corporate. Sprawl. Urban renewal: the massive destruction of historic city fabric, the construction of the interstate highway system, the reconstruction of the post-urban-renewal city. Repair. Protests: social, political, racial, and environmental. Clarke and Rapuano, Sasaki, Sasaki Walker, Sasaki Dawson and DeMay, Johnson Johnson and Roy, JJR, Halprin, Friedberg, Eckbo Dean Austin and Williams, EDAW, Kiley, Royston, Wallace McHarg Roberts and Todd, WRT, Zion and Breen, Simonds and Simonds, GWSM, Bye. Invisible landscapes. Background landscapes. Object landscapes. Contextual landscapes. Partial landscapes. Temporary landscapes. The deaths of Ellen Shipman, Beatrix Farrand, Fletcher Steele, Jens Jensen, Frederick Law Olmsted, Jr., and Elbert Peets. The changing of the guard, the adolescence of the profession of landscape architecture.

Three threads emerge out of the fabric of so many works, designers, and places: 1) the effect of automobile ownership on the postwar landscape; 2) the changes to the typology of the garden; and 3) the increasing consciousness of this era as the Age of Ecology. The automobile, the garden, and ecology are three threads that create the narrative within which we can situate individual works of postwar landscape architecture.

This paper brackets the period from 1945 to 1970, a short, late phase of modern landscape architecture, which began in the late eighteenth century. "Modern" in this usage denotes a cultural condition that extended Enlightenment philosophy and applied the production of that knowledge to the betterment of everyday life.[1] Although this usage does not denote a stylistic period, the creative and design fields were thought to be one means of this enlightened betterment. The representational and spatial innovations—as well as the political ideology—of Picturesque theory and its concomitant focus on perception and movement are the first indications of a modern sensibility in landscape design.[2] In a second phase nineteenth-century designers employed that spatial invention for social ends in restructuring the American city and suburb; these works of public landscape architecture responded to the social effects of modernization and in turn enabled new ways of living—and new social spaces—in the modern metropolis. A third phase of modern landscape architecture follows with the self-conscious exploration of new design codes and vocabularies, the phase that Renato Poggioli refers to as "modernism."[3] Hence, my naming the works of 1945 to 1970, late-modern landscape architecture. I have chosen 1970 as the year to end my comments because the last 25 years are generally considered in a postmodern cultural context, one that is self-consciously historicist and ecological—and one in which the discourses of landscape, nature, and ecology are central, rather than marginal, concerns.

The Automobile

The sprawling configuration of America's late-twentieth-century cities was sustained, if not caused, by the popularity and availability of the automobile as a primary mode of daily travel. As such, the automobile has three impacts on the practice of landscape architecture. First, its corridors for movement—roads and highways—structure the context within which construction occurs. Homes are increasingly

distant from work, further exacerbating the disjunction between the domestic realm and the productive realm. Suburbs reach out into agricultural land, connected by tentacles of interstate highways and beltways. Regional transportation systems are co-opted for local travel.

Second, the automobile actually creates opportunities for new types of landscape projects. Corporate headquarters or campuses located near the suburban homes of CEOs, shopping centers and malls, parkways and highways, and new towns become part of the portfolios of prominent practitioners of landscape architecture. Upjohn, CIGNA, and John Deere headquarters as well as Riveroaks Shopping Center, and Reston, Virginia, and Columbia, Maryland, are cultural products that depend on the automobile for their location, form, and viability.

It could be argued that many urban plazas of the period are similarly enabled by America's love of the automobile. Projects such as Constitution Plaza, Boston City Hall Plaza, Embarcadero Plaza, Seattle Freeway Park, and the Portland Open Space Sequence are on sites disrupted and cleared as a consequence of interstate-highway construction and federal urban-renewal policies. These pedestrian spaces are beholden to the highway engineer's clearing of the ground for the construction of an aerial, or subterranean, stream of unchecked speedy movement.

The third impact that the automobile has on the modern landscape is registered in a profoundly different conception of space and time. We experience a sense of displacement as we drive a number of feet above the city and stare at rooftops as a new eye-level landscape or through a concrete trench dug below the city street grid that effectively eliminates entire neighborhoods from our image of the city. And this sense of displacement is liberating. The landscape is increasingly experienced as a place of movement, of speed, of a cinematic rather than a pictorial way of seeing. Thus the automobile structures the field within which landscape architects design, supporting new types of design projects and altering the spatial and temporal experience of the landscape. It is an enabler of the practice of modern landscape architecture.

The Garden

A second thread that runs through the late-modern landscape is the typology of the garden. The juxtaposition of the automobile and the garden reveals unexpected lessons for the student of the modern. The automobile's presence in the modern landscape is a twentieth-century condition that illustrates how new technologies and machines alter the practices of moving through—and inhabiting—the landscape. The garden, in turn, offers a different means for revealing the new, the changing, the modern. Since the garden is a typology that has persisted throughout landscape history, changes in the garden's forms, spaces, uses, and meanings refract changes in the social formation within which, and for which, gardens are constructed. Transformations in the garden type are telling; they tell stories about changes both within and without, within the discourse of landscape architecture design and without in the realm of everyday life.

Even the typology of the garden, a familiar space that has been part of the practice of landscape design for centuries, is fundamentally altered by the automobile. Mellon Square in Pittsburgh, a city block as civic plaza, is actually a roof garden atop a multilevel parking garage. This sort of garden, occupying the ground

The Donnell Garden, Sonoma County, California, with pool and lanai designed by Thomas Church and his associates

vertically displaced by the stored cars of suburban commuters, proliferates as a scarcity of urban sites necessitates inventive sectional juxtapositions.

Gardens of the more familiar category, residential gardens, also face considerable changes in the postwar decades. The gardens of designers like Thomas Church and Garrett Eckbo are extremely fragile spaces, small and subject to the whims of changing owners. The best documented, such as the Donnell and the Martin gardens by Church, evidence new codes for designing and structuring elements in the garden. While designers might state that the site conditions, client need, and economy were the essential considerations when designing a garden, it is clear that other influences were also at work. Increasingly apparent in the postwar residential garden are the formal codes of abstract art mediated through the materiality and spatiality of planted forms. The compositional codes derived from the classical revival of the early twentieth century—a reliance on symmetry, hierarchy, axiality, and precedent—give way to arrangements of three-dimensional volumes asymmetrically disposed along lines or data of movement. This shift from rooms, compartments, or enclosures to fragments of overlapping space—points, lines, planes, and volumes—denotes a significant shift in late-modern landscape architecture's disciplinary affiliation toward the visual and plastic arts.

It can be argued that these canonical gardens are the exception. In most subdivisions a desire for community leads to ordinances against fences and walls. Hence, the enclosed garden is replaced by an open space. Neither public nor private, these suburban gardens are an in-between realm of manicured lawns, more symbols of domesticity than places. Their lack of boundaries, rather than ambiguous boundaries, results in the proliferation of undifferentiated spaces, invisible landscapes, and ubiquitous open—that is, empty—spaces. That the garden is an endangered space in the late-modern landscape is not wholly the fault of developers of subdivisions, or of landscape architects. The garden's position relative to the modern house has always been problematic. Colin Rowe's observation—that while the principal victim of modern architecture was the city, the first victim was the garden[4]—underscores how dependent much of modern architecture was on a romantic, fictive, untouched matrix of nature for its surround. Given the persistence and strength of this image, it is all the more remarkable that projects like the Miller Garden by Kiley in collaboration with Saarinen and James Rose's own house and garden were built. More typical in the literature are gardens built and published devoid of architectural context—because the house was nondescript or superfluous to the garden's conception.

In brief, a review of the garden suggests that while new garden hybrids result from its combination with other types, like the parking garage, or from the appropriation of the codes of contemporary abstract art, generally the garden suffers from a lack of prestige during the postwar decades. Few architects outside the Bay Area are intrigued with the concept of garden rooms attached to their houses. In fact, most houses of the period are part of speculative subdivisions that frequently prevent the building of walls or fences, a prerequisite of garden making. The exemplary residential gardens that do get designed are the laboratories for inventing new design codes deriving as much from contemporary painting and sculpture as from site characteristics and client needs. From the writing of designers of the period—whether it be James Rose, Dan Kiley, Garrett Eckbo, or Joseph Hudnut—we discern an acute interest in the medium of space as the material that allows much of the late-modern garden's inventiveness.

The Age of Ecology

What of the third thread, the emergence of ecological thinking? Since the nineteenth century such landscape architects as Olmsted, Eliot, Clarke, and Jensen have tested the limits of ecological knowledge through their landscape construction and planning. Prior to World War II Frank Waugh and Elsa Rehmann wrote in *Landscape Architecture* magazine as well as in the popular press about the role of plant ecology in garden and landscape design.[5] And since the 1970s ecological processes, principles, metaphors, and metaphysics have provided a methodological and conceptual basis for some designers of landscape architecture. So, how does ecology figure in this late-modern, pre-Earth Day period? How can the 1940s and 1950s be considered the Age of Ecology, given that *Silent Spring* and *Design with Nature* weren't published until 1962 and 1969 respectively? For an answer, let us turn to environmental historian Donald Worster. In the final chapter of *Nature's Economy: The History of Ecological Ideas* Worster establishes his historical limits with a definitive event: "The Age of Ecology began on the desert outside Alamogordo, New Mexico, on July 16, 1945, with a dazzling fireball and a swelling mushroom cloud of radioactive gases."[6] Preserving Late-Modern and Postmodern Landscape Architecture. Fifty years of landscape architecture in the shadow of that mushroom cloud. Fifty years of frantic building and rebuilding. Homes, housing, suburbs, new towns, corporate headquarters, interstate highways, shopping malls. Fifty years of productivity backed by the confidence of the society that won the war—with that bomb.

Worster identifies a growing sense of skepticism that parallels this building boom, a skepticism about the conflation of technological innovation and cultural progress. In Worster's Age of Ecology a minority voice begins to question the values that relegate nature to a resource that serves technology, to a site for the display of technology and expansion. Instead, this postwar minority voice begins ascribing to nature intrinsic values—or at least sees nature through a less anthropocentrically centered lens: A sense of limits, a concern for the interrelationships between human nature and nonhuman nature, a desire to temper development, to limit sprawl, and to advocate conservation.

Did landscape architects contribute to this minority voice, these questioners of growth, technology, and the deployment of nature for development? Clearly, not all of them, given earlier descriptions of landscape architecture's complicitous relationship with the automobile. Was late-modern landscape architecture part of the development regime that planned through the control of nature, thus employing an instrumental view of ecology? Or was the built work conceived in the hopes of checking and regulating growth and thus supporting a subversive social and ecological stance?

Weaving Together the Threads of the Automobile and the Garden in the Age of Ecology

The past fifty years have been characterized by a pace of construction and destruction—of both the countryside and the inner city—that is unparalleled in the history of civilization. This rate of change—which causes the short shelf life of all products, including design works—provides the context for understanding Lawrence Halprin's comment: "We spend thirty to forty years trying to get our projects built, and then the next ten to twenty trying to make sure that they don't get knocked down."[7]

Accompanying this rate of change is the sense of thrill and dread described by Marshall Berman in *All That is Solid Melts into Air* as one of the conditions of modern life.[8] Understanding this paradox of simultaneous thrill and dread—the thrill of new construction and the sense of anomie over the pace of change—helps us consider what forces captured the imaginations of post-World War II designers, many of whom were inspired by the changes in practice enabled by new social patterns and values and thus sought to construct new codes for designing. One of these codes, the construct "space," liberated them from the compositional codes of their Beaux Arts-derived training and from the tired debates between the advocates of the architectural garden and the wild garden (alternatively known as the "formal" and "informal" debates).[9] The construct "space" resonated with the changing spatial practices of everyday life, and as a new medium space—the vaporous, fluid stuff in between masses and forms, buildings, walls, tree trunks, and hedges—was the

tool of invention for many of the designers of the period. It is also the ground for the discourse that weaves together the three threads I identified as categorizing the works of late-modern landscape architecture: the automobile landscape, the typology of the garden, and ecological thinking.

The Spaces of the Late-Modern Landscape

We are so preoccupied with space in the late twentieth century that it is hard to imagine a design culture that was not spatially oriented. But the use of the term to describe the area between things and the sense that this area was positive, full, and palpable do not enter the English language in design criticism until the late nineteenth century. The first mention that I have found of a landscape architecture-specific discussion is a 1918 article by Charles Downing Lay.[10] By the 1930s Fletcher Steele is writing, "I care much for the shape, size, and proportion of the empty spaces of my gardens and guard them jealously. . . . Planting is chosen to bring out and enhance the size, color, and proportion of spaces."[11] The 1948 reprint of Tunnard's *Gardens in the Modern Landscape* included an essay by Joseph Hudnut, dean of the Harvard Graduate School of Design, in which Hudnut states that "gardens, like houses, are built of space. Gardens are fragments of space set aside by the planes of terraces and walls, and disciplined foliage" and that the "new aesthetic is most clearly exhibited in the new quality of space: a space free as in no other architecture from the tyranny of structure."[12]

It is perhaps the writings of James Rose and Garrett Eckbo, beginning in the 1930s, that best explain how this spatial preoccupation altered the process of design.[13] Eckbo argues that since people live in space, "the atmospheric volume immediately above this land surface,"[14] a designer should eschew two-dimensional pattern-making and preconceived compositional codes inherited from the Beaux Arts system.[15] In lieu of those tired old codes Eckbo constructs a theory of space formation that emphasizes 1) surfacing and enclosure over enrichment and 2) horizontal and vertical surfaces and planes over focal points, axes, and rooms.[16] He advocates a plastic and structural exploration of the ground and of built/green walls to create space.[17] In 1959 Eckbo clearly positions himself as a modernist who is spatially literate in this passage from Chapter Nine, "Space for Living," in *Landscape for Living*:

> The concern with isolated pictorial compositions and with two-dimensional patterns, the snare of patterns of lines which produce no three-dimensional result on the ground, is one of the roots of the present-day aesthetic and functional inadequacy of American landscape design. This is an inadequacy of incomplete site conceptions, and they are incomplete because there is no concept of space, of volume, to pull all these scattered items of pictures and patterns, site and buildings, trees and views, natural and structural elements, into a unity greater and more compelling than their mere disorganized accumulation.[18]

I offer these few passages on space as examples, not exemplars. The case for a spatial vocabulary and literacy was pervasive in the writings of the postwar period. Designers, like other artists, writers, and scientists, were involved in probing the boundaries of spatial conceptions, organizations, and strategies; or as Melanie Simo and Peter Walker observe in the preface to *Invisible Gardens,* "In modern landscape architecture, space was rediscovered as the great unifying medium."[19] The social and formal spaces of the automobile, the routines of everyday life, created a mode of spatial experience that was detached both from the phenomena of wind, cold, and discomfort associated with speed and from the phenomenal aspects of the surrounding landscape. The spaces of the interstate highway sliced through disparate parts of the city and countryside and in doing so spliced them together, montagelike, into a spatial sequence unimaginable prior to highway construction. The physical separation of suburb, corporate headquarters, and urban core was overcome through the space of unimpeded speed—the highway and beltway. Such Halprin books as *Cities* and *Freeways* describe this modern sense of space, both its destructive impact on the city and, as we expect of a modernist, the creative potential underlying this destruction.[20] Both Embarcadero Plaza and the Seattle Freeway Park exploit the creative potential of newly created spaces under and over the space of the highway.

Similarly the typology of the garden was transformed through manipulations of the new medium, space. Gardens were comprised of spaces, not rooms, and articulated by layers and screens. Their boundaries were marked, but not bounded emphatically. Often these gardens were spatial fragments of other territories—some adjacent, some removed but regionally emblematic. These spaces, horizontally defined by the ground and the ceiling of a tree canopy, flowed into their surrounds. These garden spaces, articulated by crisp detailing and grading, hovered above the animated, objectified ground planes of gardens and urban plazas.

Finally, the growing influence of ecological thinking altered both the perception and conception of landscape spaces. What Henri Lefebvre has called full spaces—spaces full of nature, natural process, and phenomena[21]—emerged out of formerly invisible areas, open spaces, undifferentiated background landscapes. The landscape of aesthetic scenery and picture-making was replaced by sites with ecological structure and phenomenal presence that preceded the arrival of the developer and designer. Space as the medium of late-modern landscape architecture. New spaces for perceiving the metropolis. New spatial experiences. Full spaces. As a group concerned with perpetuating the legacy of late-modern landscape architecture, how do we preserve space? What are the boundaries of appropriate intervention?

Preservation Implications of Spatial Conceptions of the Landscape

In this Age of Ecology an argument could be made against preserving anything having to do with the automobile landscape: It's consumptive of land, it encourages sprawl, and it isn't sustainable. And yet—shouldn't we conserve some aspect of this important postwar era that engendered an unparalleled era of confidence in the American economic system, in our leadership in contemporary art and design, in our future? Shouldn't we identify canonical, exemplary projects that characterize landscape design of this period? One corporate headquarters in each city, one suburb, one highway-related park or plaza? And perhaps then we can relegate the rest of the spaces of the automobile landscape to structural armature that will be built upon, and over, until it reaches a desirable density? Here I am reminded of Kathryn Gleason's extraordinary archeological research into ancient Rome in which

John Deere Corporate Headquarters, Moline, Illinois, Stuart Dawson of Sasaki Walker Associates

she has identified the traces of a public garden that structured the shape and space of contemporary city blocks.[22] The modern automobile landscape could become an armature for future growth.

What should we do about projects that were conceptualized as a contextual response to the regional condition made accessible by the automobile? Dulles Airport's entrance approach was planted by Dan Kiley in Virginia red cedar groves, the pioneer tree species in the Virginia Piedmont's abandoned agricultural fields. Those surrounding fields have been developed into office complexes, auto-rental facilities, and the ever-expanding parking lots of Dulles airport. Saarinen's elegant airport stretches and expands into multiple bays on each end. Is there any integrity left to the Kiley landscape, which is increasingly isolated from its contextual field? When the context of a suburban surround changes so dramatically, it is, of course, a serious threat to the integrity of the landscape work in question. But isn't it also simply the logical process of growth in an automobile landscape? Dulles Airport and other mid-twentieth-century suburban landscapes may require a scale of contextual documentation—the "surround" and the "setting" in National Park Service parlance—beyond the standards of current preservation practices. This documentation may be the only way to preserve the meaning (versus the forms and spaces) of these landscapes engulfed in change, if meaning is construed as deriving from "context," "that which explains."[23]

The spatial reconception of the modern garden raises some interesting and difficult questions for preservationists. Let me use the example of the Miller house and garden by Saarinen and Kiley, built in Columbus, Indiana, in the 1950s—first, because it is arguably one of the finest works of residential landscape architecture in the twentieth century and, second, because of Calvin Tomkins's 1995 *New Yorker* profile.[24] The Miller Garden is a series of interconnected and overlapping spaces shaped by planted forms, allées, staggered hedges, and bosques that structure a taut, flattened earthen plinth overlooking a river valley. During an interview with Tomkins, Kiley repeats an analogy that he has often employed to describe his garden spaces: "Landscape architecture should be like a walk in the woods."[25] Using trees singularly and in arranged groups, as columns, as ceiling surfaces, and transparent volumes, Kiley creates space.

How malleable is Kiley's plant palette in this spatial enterprise? A clue is provided in the following passage from Tomkins: "Years ago, Kiley made up a list of alternative plant materials, expensive and non-expensive, so that he could adjust the costs of his landscape designs without altering the designs themselves."[26] Holly trees, Japanese maple, boxwood, magnolia, and rhododendrons can be replaced with buckthorn, staghorn sumac, privet, sweet pepper bush, and viburnum. For Kiley the form of the plant, its branching structure, its leaf shape and arrangement are a means of articulating a spatial structure. Arguably future changes to the plant species may not alter the garden's integrity—if they are similar in shape, form, and space-articulating characteristics to the plants Kiley selected. I suspect that changing a Jens Jensen landscape would follow a different logic. Clearly, these sorts of decisions must be made on a case by case basis, depending on the design codes and principles employed by the designer. Still, it suggests that for certain works of modern landscape architecture, a wide range of design interventions, or what the National Park Service literature calls "rehabilitation" treatments, are possible for even the most intact and significant of modern gardens.

Another preservation issue that emerges from a review of the spaces of the modern garden concerns design vocabulary and codes of combination. Such gardens as the Donnell Garden, designed by Thomas Church and Lawrence Halprin in the late 1940s, are remarkable for their inventive design codes. The open courtyard is only partially bounded on three sides, by a bath house, a lanai, and an earthen mound. The contour of the earthen mound, four arc segments connected to form an undulating line, further fragments the enclosing gesture of this garden overlooking the salt marshes and San Francisco Bay area to the south. The surface between these complex, ambiguous boundaries is similarly fragmented, partially square concrete pavers, partially wooden deck. Floating within the gridded flat surface is a biomorphic-shaped pool and a smaller but similarly shaped grass panel on which are arranged three large rough-surfaced stones. The surreal juxtaposition of shimmery / reflective / turquoise / wet surface with the obdurate / rough / dark mass of stone, of the controlled curvilinear lines of pool and grass surface with the angular walls of the surround, of the thinness of the glass membranes between bathhouse and deck with the heftiness of the stone retaining walls is dependent on fragments of differing geometries and materials. In other words, the spatial structure here is a function of design codes and material choices. It can be argued that changes to any part would destroy the integrity of the whole. This assemblage of fragments resists addition. Unlike a compositional whole made up of parts that can absorb additions easily through a strategy of contrast—the strategy in keeping with *The Secretary of Interior's Standards*—an assemblage of parts is held in a fragile equilibrium of balance, asymmetry, and tension. Its lack of centrality, axiality, classical proportion, and the enclosure of compartmented rooms renders a garden like the Donnell highly vulnerable to change.

Ecological Spaces
The spaces of ecological thinking open up equally problematic issues for a landscape preservationist working in the late-modern landscape. Since the ecological intrinsically assumes flux, change, and time, landscape preservation of such works may be an oxymoron, as Robert Cook has so persuasively argued in his lecture at the Asheville symposium, Balancing Nature and Culture.[27] As ecological thinking— and its associated theories of plant succession, landscape ecology and connectivity,

balance and disturbance—is gradually adopted and adapted to the design and planning of select built landscapes in the mid- to late-twentieth century, preservationists will have to consider that the design integrity of such projects as the Soros garden, Sea Ranch, or the Plan for the Valleys may not require spatial consistency. In fact, if the designer intended the project's spatial structure to evolve and change, the love of the artifact will have to be sacrificed for the art of change. Clearly this issue will become even more important when we meet in twenty years to discuss the preservation of the postmodern landscape architecture of Andropogon, George Hargreaves, Richard Haag, John Lyle, and the students of such academics as Lyle, Fritz Steiner, James Corner, Anu Mathur, Kathy Poole, and Rossana Vacarrino. Still, as we focus on the works of late modernism preservationists must confront the notion that ecological design has a historical component, that ecological theory has evolved over time, and that the mid-twentieth-century designers did not have the same ecological consciousness, or knowledge, that we do today.

Hence, let's take care not to apply our environmental values to the ecological spaces of yesterday. To illustrate this point, let's return to the Miller Garden and speculate about the substitution of a different set of plants for those planted by Kiley. What if the trees were overgrown and compromising the spatial structure of the garden? Would we allow them to remain simply because they are old mature specimens? Or would we substitute a new association of plants, more fitting to this Midwestern river bank, supporting greater wildlife diversity, in other words, more ecologically suitable and sustainable? And let's imagine that we even look for plants that have the same form and space-articulating qualities of Kiley's horse chestnuts, honey locusts, arborvitae, crabapples, and maples. Is this a fitting design intervention or rehabilitation? Or is it a violation of Kiley's design codes, which are predicated on a definition of plants as space- and form-making elements, not members of an ecological plant community? And, after making this assessment, would we follow the same reasoning for a degraded urban landscape designed by Kiley, say Independence Mall in Philadelphia, that we would for a small residential garden? When looking at the late-modern landscape—and, I would argue, the early-modern landscape as well—consider the various roles that plants play in a scheme: spatial-structuring devices, habitat indicators, windbreaks, memory devices for disappearing regional landscapes, sculptural elements in their own right. We must get beyond seeing them as simply trees—or even more problematic, seeing them solely through the eyes of a late-twentieth-century environmental lens—and try to discern the role vegetation played in the design codes of the time and of the particular designer.

Another locus for our questions about the spaces of ecology are the *Guidelines for the Treatment of Cultural Landscapes*. In the description of one landscape feature, natural systems—the work of the natural-resource manager— is differentiated from the work of the landscape preservationist: "Since natural-resource protection is a specialized field distinct from historic-landscape preservation, specialized expertise may be required to address specific issues or resources found on the property."[28]

This separation of responsibilities is problematic for anyone who studies the modern landscape. Natural systems do not simply surround the project or define the context of many works of late-modern landscape architecture. Sometimes they provide the formal vocabulary for a project as in the Portland Open Space Sequence fountain plazas (1960s). Natural processes may be revealed—or activated and made more visible—through the manipulation of the ground plane as in the Soros Garden and other projects by A.E. Bye (1967). The site plan and associated building masses may be structured to exaggerate and amplify the natural structures of the site, as at Sea Ranch. The site becomes the program, generating form, structure, and meaning. Indeed, the natural systems may have been consciously disturbed by a designer's inventions as a means of initiating ecological change.

And yet the *Guidelines* currently read as if disturbance is to be avoided and thwarted in the cultural landscape. Perhaps the *Guidelines* should be reconsidered in light of the growing recognition that human action is part of ecological change and that disturbance, not balance, is a more apt metaphor and model for nature's workings. My primary point here is a simple one. The spaces of ecology are not outside the interests of some late-modern landscape architects. They should not be outside the realms of preservation landscape architects. If they are, our modern landscapes will be compromised by two separate, and unrelated, management philosophies, one conserving an artifact, or part of it, that is deemed canonical and the other conserving a surrounding, not intersecting, ecosystem, oblivious to its reciprocity with, and dependence upon, the human construction within it.

My account of this short period of late-modern works leads me toward a few tentative conclusions. Actually, they are more conundrums than conclusions. If space is the essential characteristic of modern landscape architectural design, and this is a space of flux, of movement, of sprawl and unboundedness, a space of fragments and incompletion dependent on the structure and character of its context, does this give us extraordinary license for change and alterations? Does this mean that integrity will be difficult to defend, given the current *Guidelines,* because of the amount of change to surroundings? Can the metaphors available to us in an Age of Ecology assist our understanding of the spaces of the automobile and the garden? If the urban/suburban continuum/sprawl of the late-modern landscape is conceived of as an immature ecosystem, how can we assist its evolution into a more complex, diverse system?

Responses to these questions may lead to seemingly paradoxical strategies. We may find ourselves arguing for the conservation of certain background landscapes surrounding corporate headquarters because they actually contribute to the heterogeneity of the surrounding densely developed matrices. We may find ourselves having to objectify certain works of landscape architecture, framing them away from the context that was such an important aspect of their original form and meaning. In doing so, we conserve the forms, but not the content. In doing so, we argue for certain moments of temporal freezing in a field of fluctuating, changing surrounds. We may need to destroy and rebuild a place in order to conserve its intended spatial conception, which has become degraded as plants mature. This may lead us to a late-modern landscape version of the Japanese Ise Shrine ritual, in which the same structure is disassembled and rebuilt once a generation—to conserve its soundness and to pass on building traditions to the next generation.

For me three ideas about preserving late-modern landscape architecture emerge from my own design practice, teaching, and research activities. First, most modern landscapes are about the energy, vitality, and confidence embedded in a culture of change. I suspect few designers would mind thoughtful interventions in their work, changes that were part of a conversation between one generation and another. My second observation is that these alterations are acts of design, not preservation treatments, and so these projects should be worked on—and over—by the best of our generation of designers. My third remark is actually a personal dream, that these works can be modified by talented designers building on the lessons learned from a few healthy debates about particular case studies. In the same way that Michael Graves's extension to the Whitney Museum created a fierce debate about the integrity of Breuer's design and the limits of expansion, no matter how complementary or contrasting, the preservation guidelines for this work should emerge out of a handful of highly visible public debates and thoughtful engagements about the future of these designed and built landscapes. We must not allow projects like Nicollet Mall to be altered without a national debate on the matter. Local debates are neither strong enough to sway public opinion nor capable of shaping a coherent philosophy about the significance of the late-modern landscape to our cultural heritage.

If the National Park Service's Historic Landscape Initiative is a success, won't we have a generation of postmodern landscape architects whose design processes and philosophies strike a balance between destruction and creativity and, frankly, who aren't in need of preservation guidelines necessary to prevent the modernists from bulldozing everything in sight that is old? Here, we need to view the entire preservation movement in America as part of a postmodern sensibility that is more inclusive of the past than were late-modern design and development practices. If recent trends in landscape architecture education are effective in shaping practice, won't we have a group of designers who understand that the landscape is both cultural and natural, a record of both historical and ecological change? If recent articles in the popular press are accurate, we will find ourselves surrounded by clients and a lay public who understand how attitudes toward nature are socially constructed and who value built landscapes that encode those historical cultural values in real space and time.[29] If all three of these conditions are as influential as I hope, we won't need to be just natural-resource managers or preservation landscape architects or innovative landscape architects. A good designer will be all of these things and will take a site's prior natural and cultural history into consideration as part of every design process. It's only when we designers, historians, preservationists, and site managers collectively recognize the promise of Henri Lefebvre's description of "spaces full of (both) nature and history"—of landscapes that are unique cultural products and works of art as well as fragments of natural systems—that we will overcome one of our major inheritances from the late-modern period that I care not to preserve, open space, empty space, a condition of invisibility and marginalization, neither garden nor ecosystem.

Elizabeth K. Meyer, ASLA, is an associate professor of landscape architecture at the University of Virginia, School of Architecture, Charlottesville, Virginia.

1 For a discussion of modernity as an ongoing enterprise and its relationship to the various postmodernisms, see Jurgen Habermas, "Modernity: An Incomplete Project" in *The Anti-Aesthetic*, ed. Hal Foster (Port Townsend, Washington: Bay Press, 1983), 3-15.

2 Recent scholarship on the Picturesque that discusses the intermingling of the aesthetic, the spatial, and the political includes Anne Bermingham, *Landscape and Ideology: The Rustic Tradition 1740-1860* (Berkeley: University of California Press, 1986), and Sidney Robinson, *Inquiry into the Picturesque* (Chicago: University of Chicago Press, 1991).

3 Renato Poggioli, *The Theory of the Avant-Garde* (Cambridge: Harvard University Press, 1968), 218.

4 Colin Rowe, "The Present Urban Predicament," *Cornell Journal of Architecture* (Fall 1981), 30.

5 In addition to their many articles, see Elsa Rehmann and Edith Roberts, *American Plants for American Gardens* (New York: MacMillan, 1929). Frank Waugh's writings include such articles as "The Ecology of the Roadside," *Landscape Architecture* (January 1931), 81-92, and such books as *The Natural Style in Landscape Gardening* (Boston: Badger, 1917).

6 Donald Worster, *Nature's Economy: The History of Ecological Ideas* (Cambridge: Cambridge University Press, 1977, 1985 reprint), 339.

7 Conversation between Lawrence Halprin and Charles Birnbaum, April 1995.

8 Marshal Berman, *All That is Solid Melts Into Air: The Experience of Modernity* (New York: Penguin Books, 1982, 1988 reprint), 15.

9 This debate is a continuation of the William Robinson and Reginald Blomfield debates of the late nineteenth century. See William Robinson, "Garden Design and Recent Writings Upon It," *The English Flower Garden* (New York: The Amaryllis Press, 1984 reprint of the fifteenth edition), 26-35, and Reginald Blomfield, *The Formal Garden in England* (London: MacMillan. 1936, reprint of 1892 edition).

10 Charles Downing Lay, "Space Composition," *Landscape Architecture* (January 1918), 77-86.

11 As cited in Robin Karson, *Fletcher Steele, Landscape Architect: An Account of the Gardenmaker's Life, 1885-1971* (New York: Harry Abrams/Sagapress, 1989). This citation is an excerpt from a letter from Steele to F. F. Rockwell, June 10, 1955.

12 Joseph Hudnut, "The Modern Garden," *Gardens in the Modern Landscape*, ed. Christopher Tunnard (London: Architectural Press, 1948 reprint), 175-78.

13 Eckbo's 1930 articles include "Small Gardens in the City," *Pencil Points* (September 1937), "Sculpture and Landscape Design," *Magazine of Art* (April 1938), a three-part series on "Landscape Design" in *Architectural Record* (1939-1940) co-authored with Dan Kiley and James Rose, and "Outdoors and In—Gardens as Living Space," *Magazine of Art* (October 1941).

14 Garrett Eckbo, Chapter Nine, "Space for Living," *Landscape for Living* (Los Angeles: Dodge, 1959), 61.

15 Garrett Eckbo, "American Gardens 1930s-1980s," *Process Architecture*, 90 (1990); Garrett Eckbo, *Philosophy of Landscape*, 110-13.

16 *Landscape for Living*, 64.

17 Ibid, 68.

18 Ibid, 63.

19 Peter Walker and Melanie Simo, *Invisible Gardens* (Cambridge: MIT Press, 1964), 3.

20 Lawrence Halprin, *Cities* (Cambridge: MIT Press, 1972 reprint of 1963 edition) and *Freeways* (New York: Reinhold, 1966).

21 Here I draw on the arguments of Henri Lefebvre, *The Production of Space* (Oxford: Blackwell Press, 1991 translation of 1974 edition), in which he differentiates between open space and full space, spaces full of nature and history.

22 Kathryn Gleason, "The Garden Portico of Pompey the Great: an ancient public park preserved in the layers of Rome," *Expedition* (1990), 4-13, and "Porticus Peompeiana: a new perspective on the first public park of ancient Rome," in *Journal of Garden History* (January/March 1994), 13-27.

23 *Oxford English Dictionary*, second edition, WWB interface, University of Virginia library.

24 Calvin Tomkins, "The Garden Artist," *The New Yorker* (October 16, 1995), 136-47.

25 Ibid, 143.

26 Ibid.

27 Robert Cook, "Is Landscape Preservation an Oxymoron?" lecture given in Asheville, North Carolina at the Balancing Nature and Culture symposium, April 1995; Charles Birnbaum and Sandra Tallant, "Balancing Natural and Cultural Issues in the Preservation of Historic Landscapes," *The George Wright Forum*, 13:1 (1996).

28 Draft Guidelines for the Treatment of Historic Landscapes (Washington, D.C.: U.S. Department of Interior, National Park Service, Preservation Assistance Division, 1992), 9. The final version of this document does not so emphatically separate the work and scope of a cultural landscape architect from that of an ecologist. This revision, as well as others, bring these standards closer to the design theories and practices of twentieth-century landscape architecture. See *The Secretary's Standards for the Treatment of Historic Properties with Guidelines for the Treatment of Cultural Landscapes*, ed. Charles Birnbaum and Christine Capella Peters (Washington, D.C.: U.S. Department of Interior, National Park Service, Cultural Resources Stewardship and Partnerships, Heritage Preservation Services, Historic Landscape Initiative, 1996). This paper was written before the publication of the 1996 *Standards* and has not been modified to address all the changes between the draft and final versions.

29 See, for example, Jay Parini, "The Greening of the Humanities," *The New York Times Sunday Magazine* (October 29,1995), 52-53.

Preservation and the Public
Robert Bruegmann

America's postwar palaces: the suburban corporate center. General Motors Technical Center, Warren, Michigan, Eliel and Eero Saarinen, architect, Thomas Church landscape design

The mature landscape of the urban renewal era. Constitution Plaza in Hartford, Connecticut, Charles DuBose site planing and design coordination, Sasaki Walker Associates, landscape architects

The goal of thrusting recent landscape design into the preservation arena presents certain challenges as well as opportunities. A good way to assess some of these challenges is to consider this goal in the light cast by the history of architectural preservation.

Since the beginning, the preservation movements in Europe and the United States have been marked by their respective origins. In the nineteenth and early twentieth century European preservation was often unabashedly elitist, focusing on the cathedral, the palace, and the Medieval or Renaissance city center. In almost every case these were buildings and environments created by powerful and wealthy patrons. Landscapes were saved because they were integral parts of the ensemble. In the United States early preservation efforts usually focused on buildings associated with patriots and events connected with the birth of our country. Landscape preservation, when it was considered at all, was dominated by a focus on the conservation of wilderness and the natural environment.

The preservation movement, as we know it today, was forged in the late 1960s. It joined a number of other grassroots movements concerned with the natural and built environment. Much of the emotional charge for this movement was a negative one, aimed at modernist architecture and planning ideals. Preservationists were appalled at what they considered the destruction of the city through urban renewal and highway building. They decried the replacement of gracious old buildings by insensitive, out-of-scale modernist ones.

One response, especially in Europe, was the neighborhood conservation movement. Neighborhood conservation was often achieved with relatively little controversy since it affected large areas of the city—with both benefits and costs spread widely. In places like Bologna, for example, with its socialist municipal administration, neighborhoods were conserved for the existing working-class population. The result was closely analogous to natural conservation with its focus on both setting and inhabitants.

In the United States, however, the idea of conservation in an urban context never really took root. Instead, Americans shifted their attention from the preservation of patriotic sites to the preservation of architectural art. Moreover, when districts were designated, they were often those that had been discovered by "urban pioneers" as areas suitable for gentrification. The resulting process, in which the buildings were meticulously preserved but the social life of the neighborhood totally altered as existing residents were displaced by affluent newcomers, reinforced for many citizens the association of preservation with an intellectual and economic elite. This was also true in the case of the preservation of individual buildings, for which the preferred mode of protection was the local ordinance based on the police power of the state.

Landscape preservation figured into the preservation efforts of the 1960s and 1970s, but was greatly hindered by two factors. First, because landscape was by definition always changing, defining exactly what to preserve presented fundamental philosophical problems. Second, there was an absence of basic historical research. Among landscape architects the only name that was really well known was Frederick Law Olmsted, and even in the case of Olmsted there was a notable absence of information about how his designs had actually been executed and what survived.

In recent years the field of architectural preservation has expanded dramatically. The most important expansion has been chronological. Now that we have passed the fiftieth anniversary of the end of World War II many preservationists have started thinking seriously about the preservation of postwar modernist buildings. This chronological extension has coincided with several other enlargements of the field. Preservationists are increasingly interested in the typical and the vernacular in addition to monuments of high-art architecture. There has also been an attempt to broaden the field of preservation by considering buildings and environments that provide testimony to the lives of people who were not wealthy and powerful.

These recent changes have thrown into greater relief certain problems or contradictions, many of which always existed just below the surface in the preservation movement. The first is the relationship of preservation to twentieth-century avant-garde modernism. At first glance it would appear to be a simple matter to include modernist buildings along with the works of earlier periods in the roster of buildings to save, making twentieth-century modernism one more style in the long chain of styles. To do this, however, fundamentally distorts the most basic tenets of many of the architects of these buildings, who believed that they had killed style. In some ways to "preserve" a modernist building as a historic monument does violence to the spirit in which it was created. It also means overturning many of the judgments made by preservationists only one generation ago when they picketed against these very buildings in battles against demolitions and urban-renewal projects. Of course, these buildings now look rather quaint and, with their mature landscape, contribute much to the cityscape so that, understandably, across the country preservationists are considering them for designation as historic landmarks. But how to explain to the public at large that the work that was supposedly destroying the city in one decade has become the historic monument of another?

Preservation continues to be locked in a love-hate relationship with avant-garde modernism. Although preservationists claim to have turned modernist ideas on their head, in many ways the goal has stayed exactly the same: to transform life by reforming the environment. Only the aesthetic has changed. Rather than modernist style we have preservationist style. Like modernism, preservationism has often been

PHOTOS: ROBERT BRUEGMANN

a messianic, quasi-religious, and highly intolerant undertaking. The most visible activity of preservationists has been the use of local landmark laws. These laws, in the opinion of many property owners, unfairly burden individual owners in order to create benefits for the public as a whole. As designations have multiplied there has been a sharp reaction by many individuals who believe that government intervention in preservation, like government intervention in civil rights or environmental protection, has gone too far in serving a particular special-interest group at the expense of the general good and is arbitrary and capricious in its operation. A large part of the resentment toward preservation, as well as toward natural conservation and various other reform movements, has been based on issues of class. Despite all efforts to broaden its base, preservation—in the eyes of many—remains the province of an elite.

Perhaps the most serious problem that has surfaced in recent preservation activities has been the baring in ever more obvious ways of some basic philosophical contradictions. These contradictions involve, for example, the competing goals of maintaining visual integrity and maintaining the integrity of fabric. In architecture this debate was already clearly articulated in the nineteenth century in the bitter quarrel between restorationists like Viollet-le-Duc and anti-restorationists like William Morris. Morris rejected the restorations of Viollet-le-Duc because they removed later additions in an effort to re-create the visual harmony of a given era in the past. To remove later additions to a building or to restore in any way removes history, according to Morris and his Anti-Scrape friends.

Since World War II preservationists have tended increasingly to favor the anti-scrape argument in principle but not in practice—where restoration is very common. This split between principle and practice is perhaps necessary because the Morris argument, taken to its extreme, throws into question the entire philosophical basis of preservation. If removing any piece of fabric removes part of the history of a building, does not any attempt to stop change by landmark designation tamper with the future history of the building? At the very least it often involves trying to curb exactly those forces that were responsible for the building in the first place. To protect the early skyscrapers in Chicago from today's real estate market, for example, seems completely incongruous when we remember that it was the unbridled operation of this market that was responsible for them in the first place.

While these issues were playing themselves out in historic preservation over the last several decades, primarily in the realm of architecture, the scope for landscape designers was increasing dramatically. With the enormous decentralization of the American city came some of the largest and most conspicuous landscape commissions in history. Among the grandest of these landscapes were those of such suburban corporate ensembles as the General Motors Technical Center in Warren, Michigan, by Thomas Church; the John Deere headquarters in Moline, Illinois, by Sasaki Associates, and the Weyerhaeuser headquarters near Tacoma, Washington, by Sasaki Walker Associates; and the Becton Dickinson headquarters in Franklin Lakes, New Jersey, by Morgan Wheelock. A number of developers soon found that spending money on landscape to elevate the status of a project and give it a distinctive place in the market was more cost-effective than spending the same amount of money on architecture. Even industrial parks now receive lavish landscapes.

The American Freeway as a linear park: Interstate 280 in San Mateo County, California, between San Francisco and San Jose, landscape consultant, Lawrence Halprin

Few Americans would recognize the names of the landscape architects of even the most important projects. This is probably just as well. In architecture the elevation of single creators to the status of genius, different in kind from the rest of the profession, has tended to throw all other practitioners into the shade, and the concentration on a very few supposed masterpieces has deflected attention from the rest of the built environment. Nevertheless, a desire to give landscape some of the same prestige that attaches to architecture is a worthwhile effort. No one will quarrel with the need for extensive research in the history of landscape—including its recent history—and for major efforts at public education.

Efforts to preserve landscape, however, raise many of the contradictions confronting architectural preservation. There is, for example, the same temptation to use the landmarking process so that one group or another can impose its "principles" on the built environment. If problems of integrity and defining "original condition" are difficult in art and architecture, they are almost hopelessly confusing in landscape since landscape is always in flux.

But perhaps the conceptual difficulties in defining landscape preservation will become a blessing. It may be that landscape preservationists will be able to concentrate less on "principles," which seem to change every generation, and more on public education. Perhaps the ultimate challenge is to reunite the ideals of preservation and conservation. In this way landscape architecture might realign itself with natural conservation and escape the rift that exists in architectural preservation between the desire to preserve community and the desire to preserve architectural setting. It might also head off the possibility of the kind of rift between the preservationist and the practitioner that is so visible in architecture.

Charges of elitism seem less a problem in landscape than in architecture, in part because few postwar landscape designers, even those who thought of themselves as modernists, appear to have accepted the tenets of avant-garde modernism. For this reason there has never been as much negative feeling about landscapes as there has been about many buildings. Interestingly enough, however, it now appears that a number of landscape designers, taking inspiration from contemporary sculpture and graphic design, have claimed for themselves the right to be avant-garde. Is it possible that there is a cause-effect relationship between the appearance of this avant-garde position and the recent growth of interest in landscape preservation?

The vernacular landscape: planting and objects in front of a house in working class Pittsburgh

Vanished landmarks: Old Orchard Shopping Center, Skokie, Illinois, landscape design by Lawrence Halprin, landscape destroyed 1995

What about the bias in favor of trained professionals? Most of the landscapes discussed in the context of landscape preservation have been the result of design professionals working for wealthy clients. There is often a related bias toward a kind of nineteenth-century hierarchy of artistic endeavor that favors the ornamental over the utilitarian, the garden over the working landscape. Will landscape preservation move quickly to embrace other kinds of designed environments?

One issue that confronts any preservationist dealing with postwar designs is perhaps even more acute in landscape than in architecture. This is the fact that many of the most conspicuous landscapes have been integral pieces in a process in which American cities have seen their centers destroyed and their edges developed with what critics call "sprawl," development that flies in the face of the wisdom expounded by many environmentalists. This is a major problem for the landscape profession and one that lies beyond the scope of this paper. Still, I can suggest in passing that a close study of the low-density landscapes we have created appears to show that, far from the unmitigated disaster that reformers would like us to believe they are, they may in fact be merely a different kind of urban pattern from the one we are used to.

This paper is a plea for tolerance. The worst mistake that landscape professionals can make as they approach preservation of the recent past is to follow the lead of architectural preservation, particularly the propensity to assume that the role of the preservationist is to teach people some transcendent principles that will guide them. No such principles have survived more than a generation, and, in any case, virtually every decision about land use benefits some citizens and hurts others.

Ultimately no movement can succeed for long without a broad base of support. I can only hope that landscape preservationists will learn from the failures as well as the successes of architectural preservation and engage in the activity with a little less proselytizing zeal, a little more confidence in the slow process of education and consensus building, a little less desire to make the landscape conform to any single notion of how the world should be, and a great deal more curiosity about the amazingly varied landscapes that we have actually created over the years.

Robert Bruegmann is a professor of art history, architecture, and urban planning at the University of Illinois at Chicago.

Preserving Space, Time, and the Landscape Architecture of James Rose

Dean Cardasis

Preserving the legacy of James Rose (1913-1991) is a complex matter. First, while many people are aware that Rose was one of the three rebellious students who ushered in the modern era in landscape architecture in the mid-1930s, few are aware of his accomplishments in the subsequent years. Thus, a great deal of Rose's legacy must first be researched and documented before it can be preserved. Second, Rose was in many ways the quintessential modern rebel, maverick impossible, called in *Elle Decor* "the James Dean of landscape architecture,"[1] a man whose life as well as work was subversive and explosive. Getting close to Rose and his work was a dangerous proposition. Here was a man who unleashed an attack dog on a prospective client at an initial interview, got into a fist fight with James Thurber just seconds after meeting him at a cocktail party, and generally challenged everyone with whom he came into contact. Third, Rose was a great theoretician, writing numerous articles as well as creating instructive, experimental built works. In both theory and built work Rose attempted to express the inexpressible, between-the-lines meaning of landscape. It is impossible to separate his esoteric ideas from his built works. And fourth, analogous to explorations of the meaning of modern life in painting, sculpture, dance, theater, poetry, fiction, and architecture, Rose explored a new, contemporary understanding of space and time in the art form of landscape architecture.

Rose's gardens are all about complex, subtle, multifaceted, continuous though interrupted, ever-changing modern landscape space. Thus, the issue of historic preservation itself becomes a new question, one in which the traditional effort to preserve the material qualities of objects and surfaces is insufficient to preserve the meaning of a legacy the essence of which is space and change.

Rose's work is characterized by spontaneous improvisation with the land. His gardens are intended for contemplation and self-discovery. They respond to the particulars of their sites in specific ways, often recycling raw materials found therein and incorporating such existing site features as rock outcroppings and trees as part of a designed, flexible, irregular, asymmetrical spatial geometry. Abhorring waste, Rose often reused discarded building materials and constructions originally intended for other purposes. Old doors became elegant garden benches, metal barbecues turned into fountains, railroad ties became walls for irregular garden terraces. Overall Rose's gardens are highly ordered sculptural compositions of space. They are like giant origami, the experience of which unfolds from the inside.

One of the many complex modern-landscape spatial ideas explored by Rose— "fusion," as he called it, of indoor and outdoor space—characterizes one of his most important works, the James Rose residence, now the study center. For Rose "fusion" was not only spatial but temporal. Rose lived in and used his own home as a kind of living laboratory for almost forty years. During this time he experimented with design improvisations, thereby providing us with a continuous record of the mind of one of our most important modern landscape theoreticians.

In order to explore Rose's legacy and the problems of preserving his residence it is useful to present a clearer picture of who James Rose was, focusing on some of his ideas regarding fusion as expressed in his writings from the 1930s on. Since Rose was both theorist and practitioner, the Rose residence cum study center will be examined in the context of others of his built works. This paper will conclude with a description of how the James Rose Center is wrestling with the problems of "preserving" this environment and Rose's unique legacy to contemporary environmental design.

James Rose and the Fusion of Space

Rose was born on Easter Sunday, 1913, and died on September 16, 1991, at the age of seventy-eight. James was only five when his father died, after which he moved to New York City with his mother and older sister, Virginia. He never graduated from high school (because he refused to take music and mechanical drafting) but somehow managed to enroll in agricultural courses at Cornell University and transfer, a few years later, as a special student to Harvard University to study landscape architecture. It was there he met Dan Kiley and Garrett Eckbo, and it was from there that he was summarily expelled for refusing to design in the Beaux Arts manner.

Among his other achievements Rose wrote numerous articles and four books: *Creative Gardens* (1958), *Gardens Make Me Laugh* (1965), *The Heavenly Environment* (1965), and *Modern American Gardens* (1967). After his first book, *Creative Gardens,* was published, his editor, looking for a coffee-table book, complained about Rose's thick, theoretical prose. According to Rose he demanded Rose's next book include photographs of his work but be written by someone else. This was *Modern American Gardens* by Marc Snow, which was actually written by Rose and submitted to his editor in March as a snow job. One can easily sense Rose's delight in referring to himself in the third person while describing the climate at Harvard in 1936:

> The academic smolder over abstract principles of design flamed into an open student revolt. The chief protagonists, Garrett Eckbo, Dan Kiley, and James Rose, on the student side of the drama, seem to have been alternately outraged by the academic restrictions of the Mayflower hierarchy and exultant in having such a beautifully classic adversary against whom to do battle. They experimented secretly, unbeknownst to the landscape faculty, on designs in the forbidden area of the modern idiom. These clandestine experiments were held in Cambridge rooming houses and in the basement of Robinson Hall, somewhat in the manner of early medical students dissecting corpses in secret to gain a firsthand knowledge of anatomy. Like the schoolteacher with eyes in the back of her head, Harvard, on the faculty side of the drama, knew perfectly well what was going on and was not in the least amused.[2]

By this time modernism was in full swing in the arts and architecture. In 1937 Richard Hudnut was appointed dean of the Harvard architecture school, and he appointed Walter Gropius as head of the new Graduate School of Design. Such modern luminaries as Sigfried Giedion, Josef Albers, and Marcel Breuer, to name but a few, came as visiting critics and lecturers. All this stimulation presented an irresistible force to Rose. But the landscape architecture department remained unmoved, adhering, in Rose's words, to "Beaux Arts neoclassical French and Italian style"[3] at a time when Rose was advocating an organic evolution of form deriving from the site and the problem. He threw his hands up in the air and proclaimed, "Cripes, even if you could find a site just like the Villa D'Este, where are you going to find Mr. D'Este?"[4]

In 1990 Rose recollected an incident that precipitated his expulsion: "The assignment was posted on the board and at the bottom it read, 'Anyone attempting a modernistic solution will receive an X.' Well, I did a 'modernistic' solution, got an X; did more 'modernistic' solutions, got more X's; and eventually they expelled me. I took my X's to *Pencil Points* magazine, now *Progressive Architecture,* and they gave

Spatial Fusion: the James Rose residence circa 1954

PHOTOS AND DRAWING COURTESY OF THE JAMES ROSE CENTER

me a two-year contract!"[5] These seminal articles were among the first to clearly enunciate the message of modern landscape architecture. They were written with the same verve and vitality as evidenced in Rose's built works and were devoured by young landscape architects and architects alike.

In "Integration," published in *Pencil Points* in December 1938, Rose describes a fundamental problem in the contemporary approach to designing the environment that foreshadows his own solution at his Ridgewood home.

Landscape design exists in an isolated world of never-changing aestheticism. . . . Architects have sinned more progressively. They have built a kind of scenic railway in design where anyone may get a thrill who takes the ride, but after a few nostalgic moments, the passenger is delivered to precisely the point where he got on, and whence he continues the haphazardry of his existence. With a few notable exceptions, architects have made no attempt to express any human experience outside the walls of a building. Houses are now, more than ever, designed as a special entity, wrapped in a package and delivered to the public. No matter how much they may resemble a "machine for living," they are still an *objet d'art,* and as such, may provide a momentary thrill and eventually become interesting to collectors, but at present, they have little relation to the *rest* of the world in which living also occurs.[6]

Rose summarizes by rhetorically asking, "Isn't it a little inconsistent, and perhaps, unfair, to expect a Twentieth Century individual to step out of a stream-lined automobile, and then flounder through a Rousseauian wilderness until he reaches a 'machine for living'? We cannot confine living, which is a process, to little segregated compartments that end at the edge of the nearest terrace where we are again asked to adjust ourselves to what, in its highest form, becomes an Eighteenth Century landscape painting."[7] Rose concludes his argument by calling for "forgetting the mean, little professional boundaries which we have inherited from the stagnant era, and developing continuity in our environment expressive of Twentieth Century communal needs."[8]

It was again in *Pencil Points* in an April 1939 article entitled "Plant Forms and Space" that Rose asserts, "Space is the constant in all three dimensional design, but a realization of space is not possible until it is defined by materials. In both architecture and landscape, material plus space create a volume through which human beings circulate and carry on the functions of living."[9] While Rose goes on to discuss the differences in materials for landscape and architecture, it is key to understanding the importance of Rose's approach to design to recognize that for Rose the differences between architecture and landscape were not as important as the similarities.

In this article Rose criticizes most architects' view of the landscape. " 'Ah, wilderness!,' murmurs the architect, as he looks at the panoramic view of 'billowy foliage' through a thirty-foot expanse of glass with steel supports. 'Complete wilderness,' he echoes, and the stillness is broken only by the radio and the shrill train whistle at the town station."[10] Rose continues, describing the architect as one who is "preoccupied with that which occurs within the shell of a building, and can see no justification for design which has no compulsion of shelter. He forgets that the real purpose of design is to facilitate the activity of men. He forgets that although shelter has compulsion, there is no compulsion whatever about having architects to provide it. Shelter would occur with or without architects just as the landscape is humanized wherever man goes—with or without advice from the landscaper."[11]

It would be inaccurate to claim that there were no architects dealing with the issue of integration. Perhaps first among them was Frank Lloyd Wright, whose houses are famous for their integration with their sites. "Wright himself had the great gift of making the landscape inseparable from his buildings to a degree probably equaled by no other architect of this century or in any country," writes Rose.[12] But Rose goes on to state, "Wright was not as interested in creating gardens or landscapes as he was in integrating the natural environment with the design of his houses. Certainly, he was not interested in making his houses part of a garden."[13]

Mies van der Rohe's Barcelona Pavilion and subsequent houses evidenced explorations of architectural space having an abstract relationship with nature. Again, however, we find no interest in designing the out-of-doors as a real place for modern living. Rudolph Schindler and Richard Neutra extended interior architectural space into the landscape through walls that serve as little more than vapor barriers, then designed the out-of-doors for California living. Of Neutra Rose writes, "Neutra, on the other hand, an architect of the International School, was not handicapped by landscape training at all, but rather by an enthusiasm for gardening that was irrepressible. Seldom has an architect appeared on the scene with such rigid tenets of design and building in the modern idiom. With a brilliant mind, tenacious and undeviating as a bear trap, as far as buildings were concerned, Neutra could relax utterly as a kind of antidote when it came to his gardens."[14]

Eero Saarinen's and Dan Kiley's Miller house and garden, built shortly after Rose's Ridgewood home, is a famous example of integration of interior and exterior space. Kiley describes the garden conception simply: "The house was designed in functional blocks, such as the kitchen, the dining room, the master bedroom, and the living room. So I took this same geometry and made rooms outside using trees in groves and allées."[15] These and a handful of other explorations focused on relating shelter to nature or on integrating house and garden by bringing the out-of-doors in or by extending the interior architectural logic out. The Rose residence was a fused conception of space from its outset. The distinction between inside and outside is trivial.

The Rose Environment—Integration in Space and Time

In the case of the Rose residence we find a conception of architectural and landscape space unified from the start. Furthermore, this conception acknowledges the inevitability of change in time while creating a continuous interlocking spatial experience that, in Rose's words, is "neither landscape nor architecture, but both; neither indoors nor outdoors, but both. And this may be the message held in the emptiness between the lines drawn by materials."[16]

It was a message that he continued to explore for almost forty years. Rose began the design while in Okinawa during World War II with a model he made from scraps found in construction battalion headquarters. Later he described his thinking in an article published in *American Home* magazine in 1943:

> I wanted a structural pattern as plastic as good sculpture—large and open enough to wander through. I wanted to be able to wonder whether I was indoors or out on fine cool days and yet be snugly insulated from the heat and cold. I wanted the sensations one feels in passing from concrete paving to pine needles and earth. I wanted the spaces flowing easily from one to another, divided for privacy and for convenience. I wanted the arrangement flexible and varied. Most of all I wanted all this to be integrated with the site in a design that seemed to grow, to mature, to renew itself as all living things do.[17]

His premise was "to go at the construction as you might a painting or a piece of sculpture . . . to set up a basic armature of walls and roofs, and open spaces to establish their relationships, but leave it free to allow for improvisation. In that way it would never be 'finished' but constantly evolving from one stage to the next—a metamorphosis such as we find, commonly, in nature."[18]

Rose described his residence as a "tiny village" constructed on an area half the size of a tennis court. In it Rose had a private studio on the north of the property, while his mother occupied the central part of the dwelling and his stepsister resided in the "apartment" on the south.

Consistent with his theory of flexibility, the structure changed dramatically over the next forty years. Figures Four and Five illustrate essentially the same view from the living room to the east garden, separated by forty years of living.

Temporal Fusion: the James Rose Center circa 1989

From his first real trip to Japan in 1960 (Rose did not credit his time on Okinawa during World War II with teaching him anything about Japanese culture) and during many subsequent trips Rose became interested in Japanese culture. He became a practicing Zen Buddhist. The Japanese influence on Rose was profound and is reflected in the changes the Rose residence underwent in subsequent years. It remains, however, an American environment in suburban New Jersey. (Rose once responded to a woman who asked him if he could do a Japanese garden for her with, "Of course, whereabouts in Japan do you live?")[19]

In the addition of the roof garden in the early 1970s Rose gets still more space for people from his one half of a tennis court. Here he compares the filigrees of plant forms to the filigrees of structures: "In the bare architectural outline is a pattern of organic (rather than cosmetic) decoration and an integral division of space."[20]

Preservation Issues

Rose designed and built his own home to be flexible in order to accommodate rapid twentieth-century changes in both the environment and people's needs. In the period before and immediately after his death the structure rapidly fell into disrepair. Before his death Rose set in motion an idea he had been considering for many years—to convert his home into a landscape research and study center, intended among other things to assist those struggling with the meaning of the garden in the contemporary world. It is one goal of this center to revive the Rose home cum study center without losing the vitality that created and sustained it during his life.

In this environment, based upon a fused conception of space and a full realization that the essence of all environment design is change, the issue of preservation is a new problem. Since it was Rose's insight that continuously sparked this dynamic environment, it is appropriate to look to him for guidance. Rose himself writes in 1940 in *California Arts and Architecture* of an encounter with the problem of historic preservation: "We talked a great deal about what could be done to preserve the original character. . . . And then we discovered something important. The old place had vitality because it had been produced from the necessities for vital living. . . . All that had changed, as living things do, and now we have a new problem. And so without subterfuge, we met the new conditions just as I feel sure the earlier pioneers must have done. We allowed it to grow out of the present necessities for vital living."[21]

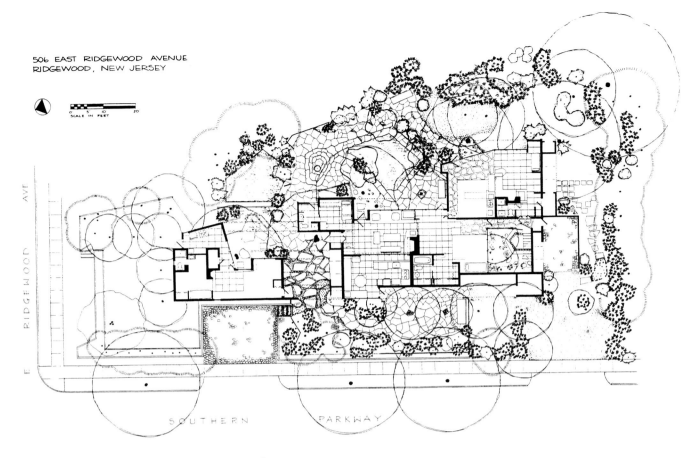

506 EAST RIDGEWOOD AVENUE
RIDGEWOOD, NEW JERSEY

First-floor plan of the James Rose Center today. Drawing courtesy of James Rose Center

Of his Ridgewood home Rose writes, "Change is the essence. To reveal what is always there is the trick. The metamorphosis is seen minute by minute, season by season, year by year. Through this looking glass, 'finish' is another word for death."[22] What I would add to this perspective would be a classical definition of "preservation," in which we only concern ourselves with halting the deterioration of objects and surfaces. Rose's design intent was that his home change with the times and needs of its users. Even after his death it is inconsistent with this intent to answer the contemporary question of how to "restore" this modern environment.

On a practical level the James Rose Center struggles with the paradoxes of preserving and perpetuating the fluidity of space and change that is at the heart of Rose's legacy. The Center has developed a flexible plan for the residence, honoring what Rose has done, but allowing for adjustments to be true to his design intent so that the functions of the Center be accommodated. Like Rose's own dynamic design for his residence, the plan is meant to serve as a framework that will be flexible enough to allow for changes but strong enough to protect what Rose created.

Sigfried Giedion writes, "History is not a compilation of facts, but an insight into a moving process of life."[23] We believe that what we are trying to preserve is a kind of living history—one that reveals the changes that have occurred over the fifty years since Rose first conceived of this environment and one that acknowledges the need for continued change if the place is to remain vital as Rose intended. Preservation of the residence becomes a question of determining how to continue to allow it to grow.

Besides developing a flexible plan, we have employed other strategies, including the following:

1. Stabilize the structure immediately

The place deteriorated quickly during the last years of Rose's life. We had to quickly identify real threats to the integrity of the environment and move to stabilize the site. We found a caretaker and the means to fund him; we also found volunteers in students and interested citizens.

In terms of actual projects we have completely rebuilt the badly leaking roof, preserved the roof garden, and repaired all the badly damaged utility infrastructure on the site. We have also preserved many of the imaginative, but severely deteriorating landscape features—for example, garden pools and fences.

2. Document the conditions of the environment at the time of Rose's death and research the history of its evolution

Since Rose kept poor records, documenting meant measuring, photographing, and quite a bit of intense nosing around. This was accomplished with the help of some excellent students from the University of Massachusetts, and a good description of this tiny but complex environment has been assembled.

3. Court allies at all levels

We alerted the Garden Conservancy, the University of Massachusetts and other universities, and the National Park Service's Historic Landscape Initiative as well as local officials and citizens to the significance of the work and the urgent need for their help. It is essential to seek help at all levels—national, regional, and local. Rose alienated virtually everyone with whom he came into contact, including many of his own clients, yet there is unquestionable merit in his work, and many people are ready to acknowledge it and do what they can to help.

4. Promote the reputation of James Rose and the importance of the Rose residence/ study center as a cultural resource

We are doing this through conferences, articles, and various outreach activities within the profession, such as our student-design awards program and the sponsorship of scholarly research; we also promote Rose's reputation with the general public through tours, open houses, and publications.

5. Research the rest of Rose's legacy and establish an archives of his work

Research is not an easy task because Rose kept few records. It is essential not only to understand, preserve, and perpetuate the physical manifestations of Rose's work but their theoretical and philosophical underpinnings as well. One important way to proceed is to encourage graduate research. Universities with graduate programs in landscape architecture are an untapped resource that can be channeled into useful, inexpensive, and productive research.

6. Document Rose's work

In 1992 we began the James Rose Documentation Project. Rose's method of working is best described as spontaneous improvisation with the land. As a result there are very few records of his built works. To date we have thoroughly documented twenty previously unknown important modern American gardens by James Rose by surveying, measuring, photographing, interviewing, and videotaping. We are in the process of planning an exhibition of this work.

7. Reach out to Rose's clients

We have tried to support and enlist the support of Rose's clients. In some cases, repair, restoration, and perpetuation of his projects have met with success, largely due to the good will of clients or the inheritors of his gardens. We have expanded our educational program to include a lecture series and student internship and awards programs at different landscape architecture schools. We are currently analyzing the possibility of establishing a library of modern landscape history at the site.

8. Seek designation in the national and state historic registers

We are optimistic that National Register status will help us maintain the integrity of Rose's vision. Our first application was made to the New Jersey State Historic Preservation Office in the fall of 1997. Designation is still pending.

9. Fund-raise

Rose left an endowment sufficient to carry on our day-to-day activities. We have stabilized the structure and made minor repairs. But major capital investment is needed. We are seeking grants and working in many small ways to raise funds through book sales, tours, benefit dinners, and—soon—a membership program.

Conclusion

It is important to preserve the spirit that created this unique modern environment. If we are to develop meaningful approaches to preserving our modern landscape heritage, we need to view the recent past through a more dynamic lens than that of traditional historic preservation. In the case of the Rose environment and legacy, predicated as they are upon important modern design theories, including those of continuity and fusion of space and time, it is critical to research both the theory and the built work. In adjusting our contemporary view of preserving the recent past and of what it means to design on the land today, it may encourage us to note Rose's appraisal of his own times written in the 1940s:

> We have begun the expression of a new age which has all the dignity and some of the greatness of ancient Greek, Medieval and Renaissance art. It is nevertheless based on a different social order and a different source of inspiration. It therefore must be judged by different standards. When thinking and living become completely unified in the process, it will be an indigenous expression of our times with fair opportunity of surpassing any of the previous periods in stature and quality. We must first know and live within our own civilization, rather than beam at it intelligently, like the faces in a cozy painting. We must get rid of the almost unconscious snobbishness which makes us imagine we are getting 'culture' at the opera while completely blind to the inventive miracles of the amusement park and the department store. When we look at things again with a fresh view rather than that of an art catalogue, we will know instinctively when to laugh and when not to laugh at Picasso, and how to build our gardens.[24]

And how to preserve—and perpetuate—our recent dynamic modern landscape heritage.

Dean Cardasis, ASLA, is a landscape architect, an associate professor in the Department of Landscape Architecture and Regional Planning, University of Massachusetts, Amherst, and the director of the James Rose Center for Landscape Architectural Research and Design.

1 Katherine Wiltside, "Zensational," *Elle Decor* (October / November 1995), 218.

2 Marc Snow, *Modern American Gardens: Designed by James Rose* (New York: Reinholt, 1967), 17-19.

3 James C. Rose, interview with the author, July 1991.

4 Ibid.

5 Ibid.

6 James C. Rose, "Integration," *Pencil Points* (1938), 759.

7 Ibid.

8 Ibid, 760.

9 James C. Rose, "Plant Forms In Space," *Pencil Points* (April 1939), 227.

10 Ibid, 228.

11 Ibid.

12 Snow, *Modern American Gardens*, 78.

13 Ibid.

14 Ibid, 81.

15 *Modern Landscape Architecture: A Critical Review,* ed. Marc Treib (Cambridge: MIT Press, 1993), 233-34.

16 James C. Rose, *The Heavenly Environment* (Hong Kong: Athens Art Publishing, 1987), 96.

17 Ibid, 90.

18 James C. Rose, *Creative Gardens* (New York: Reinhart, 1958), 111.

19 James C. Rose, *Gardens Make Me Laugh* (Norwalk, Connecticut: Silvermine Publishing, 1965), 21.

20 Rose, *The Heavenly Environment,* 112.

21 James C. Rose, "Bogeys in the Landscape," *California Arts and Architecture* (1940), 27.

22 Rose, *The Heavenly Environment*, 106.

23 Sigfried Gideon, *Space, Time and Architecture: The Growth of a New Tradition*, 5th ed. (Cambridge: Harvard University Press, 1967), 14.

24 James C. Rose, "Gardens," *California Arts and Architecture* (1940), 20.

Dan Kiley's Site Design
for the Gateway Arch
Mary V. Hughes

This paper explores the implications of applying historic preservation theory and practice to contemporary landscapes by focusing on a case study involving the site surrounding the Gateway Arch at the Jefferson National Expansion Memorial in St. Louis, Missouri. Since the early 1990s the National Park Service (NPS) has been wrestling with difficult decisions related to the long-term maintenance of the ninety-one-acre memorial landscape, designed by Eero Saarinen and Dan Kiley between 1948 and 1964 and constructed in phases between 1971 and 1981. Working from the hypothesis that the Memorial landscape had the same significance as its more prominent centerpiece, the Arch itself, the NPS applied its preservation principles to the study of management alternatives perhaps more rigorously than has been done with any other contemporary work of landscape architecture.

To accomplish this goal the NPS prepared a cultural landscape report for the Memorial landscape, hiring a historical landscape architect, Gina Bellavia, to prepare the report with input from various parties including Kiley himself. Fortunately Kiley was enthusiastic about the project from the beginning; the Memorial was the first large commission he received after opening his own practice after World War II, and he was eager to clear up some of the lingering misunderstandings about his role in the design. The opportunity to interview the designer and review his files has helped immeasurably to clarify the evolution of the Memorial landscape. Furthermore, it was important to solicit his opinion on potential modifications to address postconstruction problems. It is important to realize, however, that the designer's own memory of his work—however compelling his anecdotes—was not infallible. The project also benefited from the critical analysis of Gregg Bleam, whose experience both as a designer in Kiley's office and as a scholar who studied Kiley's design career, allows him to evaluate the project in the context of Kiley's larger career and design philosophy. Moreover, the park managers and maintenance staff played an important role in developing solutions to the problems they dealt with on a daily basis.

The first step in the preservation planning process involved thorough documentation of the site and its current conditions. At the outset of the project we were surprised at how little was known about the history of the Memorial landscape design. While volumes have been written about the design and construction of the Arch itself, Kiley's role in designing the landscape has been ignored. Fortunately there was a wealth of primary source information from which to reconstruct the chronology for the landscape design: plans and drawings from both Kiley's and Saarinen's office files, project correspondence, meeting minutes, as well as interviews with Kiley, Kevin Roche, and their office staff who worked on the project. This research demonstrated that Kiley played an important role from the outset, having served as a member of Saarinen's team in the 1947-1948 design competition. After winning the commission, Kiley and Saarinen worked closely together in refining the site design over the next sixteen years. During this time many versions of the site plan were developed, and the landscape design gradually changed from the original concept of the symbolic forested "wilderness" represented in the competition drawings (Figure 1) to the more open lawn areas with reflecting pools that characterize the site today (Figure 2). Kiley's involvement with the project ceased after NPS acceptance of the design-development drawings in 1964. At this point an in-house staff of landscape architects at the San Francisco Planning and Service Center (and later the Denver Service Center) assumed control of construction-document preparation and construction supervision.

Figure 1. Original concept of the symbolic forested "wilderness"

Figure 2. The site with open lawn areas and reflecting pools

To further complicate matters some of the construction documents were subsequently prepared under contract by the St. Louis firm of Harland Bartholomew and Associates. Construction was accomplished in phases from 1971 to 1981.

The next step in the planning process was to gather information on existing site conditions, particularly with regard to situations that have caused difficult maintenance problems over the years since construction. High on this list of maintenance woes is the monoculture of more than 900 ash trees planted in tree grates along the walkways. Disease and insect problems with these trees provided the initial catalyst for the entire project, which was undertaken in response to a proposal to replace the ash with a mixed planting of various species arranged in a more naturalistic grouping in the lawn areas outside the walkways. This potentially radical change to the landscape design provoked serious consideration of the significance of the original design. The NPS brought in specialists (a pathologist, an entomologist, and a soil scientist) to consult on the tree problems. They determined that the trees' declining health is mainly caused by poor soil conditions rather than acute insect and disease

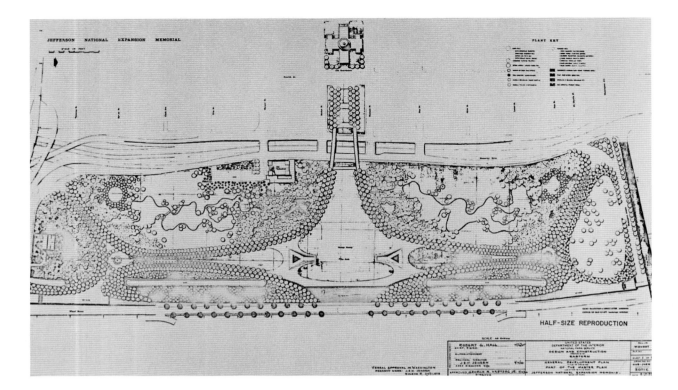

HALF-SIZE REPRODUCTION

Figure 3. The approved plan adopted by the NPS in 1966

problems resulting from the monoculture planting, as was previously thought. The tree grates themselves are another major area of concern. Located half in lawn and half in pavement, they constitute a tripping hazard and require frequent weeding. The significance and integrity of the landscape design was evaluated by comparing the historic record with the existing conditions of the site.

Although the use of the term "historic" with respect to contemporary designs may seem contradictory to some, the architectural significance of the Arch has long been acknowledged. Although the Jefferson National Expansion Memorial is less than fifty years old, it was listed on the National Register of Historic Places in 1966, only a few years after its construction, and designated a National Historic Landmark in 1987. The historical significance of the Memorial landscape, like the structure, is clearly tied to National Register criterion C, which applies to "properties significant for their physical design or construction, including such elements as architecture, landscape architecture, engineering, and artwork."[1]

The Memorial was the first major public design commission for Saarinen and Kiley, both of whom went on to achieve international reputations. Moreover, this was the first major collaborative project the two men undertook, and the relationship they established in the St. Louis project set a precedent for their continued association in future years. Project correspondence reveals that Saarinen and Kiley worked very closely together during the design process and that Saarinen's office continued in the same pattern after the architect's untimely death in 1961.

This relationship resulted in a design that integrated architecture and landscape, reflecting the holistic approach to design that Saarinen described in a 1961 interview: "I see architecture not as the building alone but the building in relation to its surroundings."[2] Saarinen played an active role in the development of the site plan: He was responsible for the design of the railroad cut that runs across the site, the layout of the walks reflecting the curvature of the Arch, and the site grading. But Kiley conferred with Saarinen on all phases of the design in a collaboration so close it is impossible to separate one designer's contribution from that of the other.

The area that appears to have been most fully Kiley's contribution was the development of the planting plan, which reinforced the geometry of the walks. The evolution of this site plan between 1948 and 1964 occurred over the years in which Kiley was maturing as a designer, developing a preference for the geometrically ordered landscape that is manifested in his major work.[3] During this period the landscape design at the Arch became much more spare and simplified, as some elements from the original competition program, such as the frontier village, the symbolic Oregon and Santa Fe trails, and the tea house and restaurant, were dropped from the site plan. In the 1960s the site design focused more narrowly on providing a functional circulation system of walkways, and a dense line of regularly spaced trees in the walks replaced the more naturalistic woodland represented on the competition drawing.

Given the lengthy and complex process of design and construction on this project, the question of historical significance largely hinges on the issue of integrity, the degree to which the built landscape reflects the Kiley-Saarinen vision. Indeed, the marked differences between the forested landscape depicted in the 1948 competition drawings and the design as finally constructed have led many people to believe that the "original" design was never built. Kiley's frequent assertions over the years that the NPS radically altered his design have further confused the historic record, as in the 1995 *New Yorker* article in which Calvin Tomkins states that "Kiley was taken off the job (over Saarinen's vigorous protests), and the National Park Service eviscerated his landscape design."[4] At Saarinen's insistence Kiley remained on the project team through the completion of design-development drawings (1964), which became the approved plan adopted by the NPS in 1966 (Figure 3). However, NPS Director Conrad Wirth—himself a landscape architect—insisted on using NPS landscape architects to produce the construction drawings. The NPS design team, led by landscape architect John Ronscavage, fully intended to implement the approved plan as faithfully as possible—although they were instructed not to contact Kiley directly for fear of incurring consulting fees.[5] However, factors beyond their control led to changes in the plan during the next ten years during which construction was implemented in phases because of a lack of funds.

The first phase of construction, completed in 1970-1972, involved overall site grading, sidewalks, and tree plantings along the north-south axis. When the contract went out for bid, local nurserymen objected to the selection of tulip poplar trees on the grounds that they did not thrive in the St. Louis climate and were not readily available at area nurseries.[6] Kiley had originally specified the dense monoculture planting of tulip poplars because of their growth characteristics: "I wanted something that soared up, cathedral-like with big, high trunks. . . . I thought the scale of the Arch being 600 feet, an 80-foot tree would be in good scale and give you an elevated feeling, too . . . a classic, spiritual feeling."[7] In developing the planting plan, his office staff wrote a series of letters to area horticulturists asking about the hardiness of material on the proposed plant list; the only negative feedback they received on the tulip poplar selection was the remark that the trees tend to drop their leaves early in the fall.[8] Because of the strong reaction of the local nurserymen, however, the NPS formed a committee to select an alternate species. This group recommended the use of Rosehill ash, a new white ash cultivar, as a replacement for the tulip poplar. Selection of the replacement variety was apparently based on hardiness and availability rather than aesthetic considerations since the height of the ash is much lower and the form of the tree more rounded and spreading than the vertical tulip poplar. Kiley was not consulted about the replacement species and recounts that he was "appalled" to hear they had chosen the ash, a tree he considers most "uninteresting."[9] The revised drawings retained the recommended spacing of the trees and the concept of a single species from Kiley's plan.

The local committee also recommended other changes to the original plant list, such as replacing the specified Canadian hemlock with Austrian and white pine. When the firm of Harland Bartholomew and Associates was retained to prepare construction documents for subsequent phases of landscape work, they were instructed to select material from the revised plant list, as modified by the local committee.[10] In later phases of construction documents, the number of trees in the lawn areas outside the walks was reduced by half from Kiley's plan.[11]

Site details and furnishings generally do not reflect the intention of the original design team. The tree grates surrounding the Rosehill ash in the walks also represent a departure from Kiley's original design, which included a strip of cobblestone between the walk pavement and the grass lawn. Apparently the park superintendent objected to the appearance of the cobbles while they were being installed and ordered them replaced with tree grates. Although the location and the alignment of the walks follow the design development plan precisely, the material was never specified.[12] The NPS design team chose the exposed aggregate concrete found at the site today.[13] The light fixture that was installed at the site was also selected at a later time by the designers at Bartholomew's office in preference to the luminaire Saarinen and Kiley had selected.[14] Other changes include several expensive items that were never built because of funding constraints, such as the overpasses over Memorial Drive, two fountains, the grand staircase to the riverfront, and the maintenance building, which continues to be housed in a temporary metal structure instead of the more inconspicuous earth-sheltered building originally planned. Instead of the surface parking lot Kiley had designed, a parking garage was built to accommodate more vehicles. Both the garage and maintenance buildings were built in the locations specified by Kiley.

Figure 4. Walkway canopy of white ash

In spite of the length of time over which the landscape plans for the Memorial were developed and implemented the Saarinen-Kiley concept, as represented in the 1964 design-development drawing, is largely that found on the site today. Despite the change in plant material the basic configuration of the Memorial landscape is faithful to the designers' intent. National Register criteria recognize seven aspects or qualities that define the integrity of a historic property: location, design, setting, materials, workmanship, feeling, and association.[15] Of these, the Arch grounds possess integrity of location, design, setting, feeling, and association. Materials and workmanship are the two categories most subject to change during the lengthy and complicated construction process. While the substitution of more than 900 tulip poplar trees with white ash alters the scale of the walkway canopy, from the pedestrian's point of view the experience is much the same as originally designed (Figure 4.) Furthermore, it is the overall concept that is of paramount importance on the ninety-one-acre site: the circulation system that reflects the gentle curvature of the Arch, the spatial quality of open lawn areas framed by dense tree plantings, the views of the Arch structured by the plantings and reflected in the lagoons, the grading that subtly screens the railroad line and service functions, and the bold simplicity of the planting plan through use of a single dominant species to reinforce the geometry of the walks. Kiley himself feels that the most important aspect of the design is the alignment of the walks, reinforced by the dense tree plantings, and the sketches found in the Saarinen archives are an indication that the architect felt the same way.[16]

A treatment plan was developed, based on the analysis and evaluation of the landscape. As a technical term "treatment" refers to work carried out to achieve a historic preservation goal. The Secretary of the Interior recognizes four basic philosophical approaches to treatment: preservation, rehabilitation, restoration, and reconstruction. We chose the rehabilitation treatment, which accepts the full evolution of the design as it was realized during the 1948-1981 period of significance while allowing for the modifications needed to solve the problems that have developed over the decades of visitor use. The plan distinguishes between those site features that have a high level of significance and integrity through association with the Kiley-Saarinen plan, such as the alignment of the walks and their monoculture planting, and those that do not, such as the benches and light fixtures. The treatment plan provides for long-term preservation of the site's significant character-defining features while allowing flexibility in altering those elements that are less important and more problematic, such as the tree grates. The NPS later brought these issues to Kiley's attention and documented his thoughts and recommendations in a taped interview at his office in Charlotte, Vermont, in July 1995.

The process of planning for the rehabilitation of the Memorial landscape has demonstrated several issues regarding the preservation of contemporary landscapes and landscapes in general. First, it is easy to be overwhelmed by the amount of information and detailed documentation for these recent projects as well as by the barrage of personal testimony, often contradictory. For works that have not stood the "test of time," it is particularly difficult to establish significance by objective criteria. For example, the case for the significance of the design concept developed by the Saarinen-Kiley team is strong while that of later modifications is less clear. Since it appears that these changes were made on a case by case basis without reference to the holistic vision uniting architecture and landscape that was the strength of the original design intent, these altered features are viewed as less significant than those that have a higher level of accord with the original designers' intentions. It is recognized, however, that future generations may have a different perspective and, therefore, a different assessment of significance.

This case study also suggests some of the ways in which preserving landscapes is different from preserving buildings. The historic preservation field, evolving over the years out of a concern for preserving architecture and artifacts, has developed a bias toward material conservation, placing an emphasis on retaining "historic fabric" with a lower regard for the less tangible qualities of place- and space-making. By these traditional standards the Memorial landscape is not historically significant because the materials found on the site today have only the most tenuous of connections to either "master" designer. Yet this judgment would ignore the fundamental fact that the Memorial integrates landscape and structure through a single powerful artistic vision that transcends individual details and materials by the strength of its underlying spatial and symbolic qualities. If it is to encompass landscapes adequately, the historic preservation field will need to become more comfortable with notions of concept, space, and other more intangible but no less real qualities of the built environment as well as with the dynamics of change

and connection to surrounding natural systems. Landscapes, after all, are often experienced more as "ground" (no pun intended) than as "figure"; spatial characteristics—proportion, scale, visual relationships—are the basic building blocks of landscape experience. The Memorial landscape, in which the design concept is more significant than individual material components, provides a dramatic illustration of these issues. As the daring design of the Jefferson National Expansion Memorial broke conventions in the fields of architecture, engineering, and landscape architecture, so will its preservation serve as an innovative model for the emerging field of historic landscape preservation.

Mary V. Hughes, ASLA, served as the historical landscape architect with the Midwest Field Area of the National Park Service. She is currently the University Landscape Architect at the University of Virginia, Charlottesville, Virginia.

1 *National Register Bulletin 15: How to Apply the National Register Criteria for Evaluation* (Washington, D.C: U.S. Department of the Interior, National Park Service, Interagency Resources Division, 17.

2 Eero Saarinen, interview in *Perspecta*, (1961), 32.

3 Gregg Bleam, "The Work of Dan Kiley," *Modern Landscape Architecture: A Critical Review*, ed. Marc Treib (Cambridge: MIT Press, 1993), 237.

4 Calvin Tomkins, "The Garden Artist," *The New Yorker* (October 16, 1995), 141.

5 John Ronscavage and Jim Holland, interview with Gina Bellavia, November 15, 1994, Denver, Colorado.

6 Ibid.

7 Dan Kiley, interview with Bob Moore, July 23, 1993, The Office of Dan Kiley, Charlotte, Vermont.

8 The proposed plant list was sent by Joe Karr of Dan Kiley's office in May 1963 to local horticultural experts requesting feedback on the proposed plant material. Advice was solicited from the following: The Morton Arboretum; Harland Bartholomew and Associates; St. Louis Department of Parks, Recreation, and Forestry; and the Missouri Botanical Gardens. Only Eldridge Lovelace of Harland Bartholomew, in a letter dated May 23, 1963, responded with negative comment about the tulip poplar.

9 Dan Kiley, interview with the author, June 8, 1991, The Office of Dan Kiley, Charlotte, Vermont.

10 Eldridge Lovelace interview with Gina Bellavia, December 1994, St. Louis, Missouri.

11 Ronscavage interview, 1994.

12 In a letter dated March 25, 1963, from Saarinen's office to Robert Hall of the NPS Eastern Office of Design and Construction, Robert Detmers discussed the use of water-bound macadam, a form of crushed stone pavement, for the walks and suggests developing test panels on-site before making a final decision about the paving material. There is no evidence the test panels were constructed.

13 Ronscavage interview, 1994.

14 Ibid.

15 *National Register Bulletin 15*, 44.

16 Kiley interview with the author, 1991.

The Landscape of the United States Air Force Academy

Duane Boyle

Air Force Academy, Colorado Springs, Colorado

West Point, the Naval Academy at Annapolis, the Coast Guard and Merchant Marine academies all have their own traditions. By contrast, the United States Air Force Academy near Colorado Springs is relatively new, and yet it could not have had a better start in setting the foundation for its own heritage. The United States was the most powerful nation in the world. World War II was over. The Cold War was heating up. An independent Air Force was established, and the Air Force Academy was a top agenda item for Congress. The prevailing attitude among Air Force leaders was that the new Academy would be different from the others—free from the burden of the past and with an eye toward the opportunities of the future.

The idea of a new military academy that would be built from scratch also came along when modernism was still in vogue. The modernist belief in technology and its promise for the future ultimately resulted in the design and construction of one of the United States government's most visible projects in the 1950s, one that is significant because of its architecture and visionary planning. Skidmore, Owings and Merrill (SOM) was chosen over Frank Lloyd Wright for, among other reasons, their track record with large projects. And Dan Kiley, SOM's landscape consultant, was to make a remarkable impact on the final design and the integration of major landscape elements with the architecture.

The setting for the Academy is dramatic. Set at the base of the Rampart Range of the Rocky Mountains, the site consists of a series of valleys separated by mesas that extend from the adjacent mountains. At the south end of the Academy a grassy plain is the center of flight-training activity. The elevation changes from 6,400 feet to 7,500 feet above sea level with the most highly developed land (the Cadet Area) at 7,200 feet above sea level. The region is classified as a high desert with temperatures ranging from the low teens in the winter to the high nineties in the summer. There is almost no humidity, and winds are common, with some gusts approaching 110 miles per hour. The high altitude, low humidity, and sunny weather make the sky an integral part of the setting, appropriately enough at a place dedicated to aviation leadership. But because of the altitude, temperature swings, and other environmental extremes planting conditions are difficult at best.

Today there is a strong feeling among staff at the Academy that good stewardship is important and that it is up to us to establish future preservation guidance. Unfortunately we learned the hard way. In the 1950s there was a debate between the Air Force and the Army Corps of Engineers about who would manage the design and construction of the Academy. The Air Force did not have its own construction agency and relied heavily on the Army and Navy to provide those services. For the Academy the Air Force wanted to manage the design and construction itself. After a hard-fought battle Congress approved the creation of the Air Force Academy Construction Agency with a life span that ended with the completion of the last Academy building, the Cadet Chapel. All subsequent projects would be managed by the Corps of Engineers.

This decision had two impacts. First, design and planning left the control not only of the Academy but also of the Air Force. And, second, the Academy had little staff expertise in design and planning—and certainly not in landscape architecture. This lack of experience and lack of attention led to a dramatic, albeit gradual, slide in quality. In particular, the impact was devastating to the original plan and landscape concept. Such important landscape elements as Kiley's ravine, which brought nature into the modernist Cadet Area, were lost. The Air Garden fountains were filled in because of perceived maintenance problems. Trees were lost and never replaced. These changes to a landscape plan that was never fully implemented caused problems that persist today.

At first the higher-level positions at the Academy were predominantly filled by West Point graduates who had transferred to the Air Force. But in the early 1980s more Air Force Academy graduates returned to the Academy in areas of responsibility. As they returned so too did a sense of ownership of the institution along with a realization that there was little control over the planned environment. During this period the staff in the Academy Civil Engineering Department was increased, a planner and several architects were hired, and the Academy began to reestablish the master plan and design guidelines.

What had been lost throughout our planning process, however, was an adequate understanding of the importance of the landscape. Only in the 1990s did it become obvious that the landscape environment needed as much, or perhaps more, attention than the architecture did.

There are two significant parts to the Academy landscape: the natural and the man-made. Each relies on the other. The 19,000 acres of the Air Force Academy are located on finger mesas that extend from the mountains. Each developed area is geographically separate, with natural transitions between developed ridges. Roadways are located on the tops of ridges or in the valleys to avoid cuts through the hillside. The Academy boundaries were located so that ridges at the north and south block the view of encroachment. The eastern boundary was located so that Interstate 25 runs on Academy property, and the Academy owns buffer land on the opposite side of the highway, again to hold off encroachment. The western boundary is a National Forest and presumably safe.

The Colorado front range is one of the fastest growing areas of the country. One recently published statistic indicates that land is being consumed for development at a rate of one acre per hour. Colorado Springs has reached the southern Academy boundary. The city has also annexed several major sites to the east, and development plans are under way for those areas. Large areas of housing are also under construction north of the Academy. Ultimately, Academy land will

A model of the Air Force Academy by Skidmore Owings and Merrill shows the strong geometry.

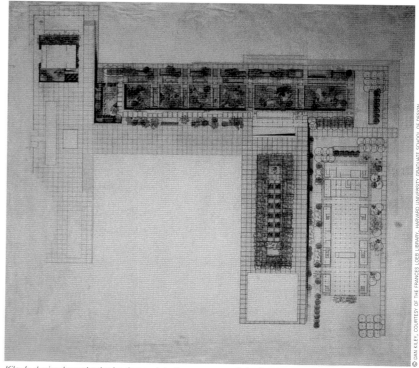

Kiley's design brought the landscape into the geometry of the Academy.

© DAN KILEY, COURTESY OF THE FRANCES LOEB LIBRARY, HARVARD UNIVERSITY GRADUATE SCHOOL OF DESIGN

be an island. At this point the value of the land will be at its highest, making it desirable to sell off the surrounding acres. It is also the point at which the value of open space will become an issue.

This problem demands a multifaceted approach. A coalition of local, state-wide, and national groups that will provide support for preserving the natural landscape is being formed, and consultants have been hired to study the value of Academy land. The Academy in essence provides 19,000 acres of open space to the local community. With the continued development of the front range any loss of Academy land diminishes the quality of life for the community and the region. To conduct our own economic evaluation of our open space and scenic vistas we have hired a team from the University of Colorado that is headed by economics professors from the Graduate School of Public Administration. They are building an economic model for the protection of the land, based on the concept of "marginal economics." The study will be part of a public relations initiative that will show the community that the natural landscape has value.

In discussing the man-made landscape at the Academy, and specifically Kiley's work, we must remember that the original landscape plan was extensive, comprehensive, and never implemented in its entirety. The tree-lined roads, the enclosure of the athletic fields, and the curvilinear landscape of the dormitory shown on the design sketches were never realized. What did get built was the ravine, the plaza, and the beautiful Air Gardens, a twenty-seven-acre oasis of concrete-and-marble paving.

To characterize what the Academy is trying to do with its modern land-scape as 'preservation' is not entirely correct. We are rebuilding. The Academy has remained a pristine example of modernism. Even today's new buildings are being designed as International Style facilities. But the landscape has not fared so well. On the one hand, the new development has not displaced any of Kiley's concept (except for the removal of the ravine). On the other hand, the landscape has not been maintained and is disappearing due to neglect and the harsh climate. In our attempt to keep acres of grass green we have drowned the trees. And when they died we have not replaced them. Most tragically, the Air Garden fountains and reflecting pools have been filled in because no one wanted to maintain them.

It is not surprising that this has occurred. In most large bureaucracies, especially those that are military- and also engineer-based, buildings are popular because they host a lot of activity and satisfy specific mission requirements. There is even some understanding of good architecture. But landscape is fluff, something that is done when extra funds are available (which they never are). Things changed, however, when the Academy received as superintendent a three-star general who was the first Air Force Academy graduate to have the office. He graduated at the top of the first Academy class in 1959 and went on to be a Rhodes Scholar. He had a firm belief that the landscape, whether natural or designed, was important to the physical plant and to the quality of life. Upon learning that the reflecting pools had been filled in and that the plant materials had deteriorated, the superintendent asked that a plan be developed to restore the cultural landscape to the fullest extent possible.

The resulting plan, which deals with the arrival at the Cadet Area, the parking-lot landscape, perimeter landscape, plazas, and the Air Gardens, is based on Kiley's concept drawings. It specifically selects tree species, irrigation type, and soil treatment/composition and also makes recommendations for reconstructing the reflecting pools.

The cost is high. The plan projects costs at $20 million to restore the Cadet Area. Although some of this can be funded by the Department of the Air Force over a period of several years, it is doubtful that such larger items as the Air Gardens will ever be restored by money appropriated by Congress. Realizing this, the Academy is now beginning to look at alternative methods of funding—for example, donations. Some projects like the reflecting pools would make good class gifts. Grants also seem a previously neglected opportunity.

Concurrent with the plan, we took one major step in restoration. We decided to look at what it would take to rebuild the fountains at the north and south ends of the Air Garden in their original configuration. There was little to go by, only the information that they had been filled in and sodded over in the 1970s. We had no record of how it was done, whether the tanks were still intact, and, if they were, what condition they were in. Most people doubted that it was feasible to restore the fountains without starting anew. Nevertheless, we very carefully used a front-end loader to remove the sod and dirt. At first the results were not encouraging. But as the excavation continued, the tank appeared in good shape with no cracking or other deterioration to the concrete. At the bottom of the tank the glass underwater lights were still unbroken, and the nozzles were intact. The underground pump room was still usable. We uncovered the electrical pull boxes which had been unused for twenty years, and they were still clear. Even the breaker panel in an adjacent building still had the original tie-in for the power. The main concerns were rebuilding the top of the vertical walls to match the original detailing and providing new pumping equipment. Resurrecting the fountains was feasible, although not simple. It was an opportunity to start the renovation of the entire Air Gardens. After a four-month construction period that was constantly hampered by bad spring storms the fountains were reactivated. It is interesting to note that the cadet pranks that centered around the original fountains are also back.

In contrast to this success dying trees remain a problem. Many of the original trees were honey locusts. These trees worked well with the architecture since they have a feathery leaf that buffers but does not hide the buildings. These trees are also at the maximum elevation they can tolerate. Those that are sheltered still do well. Those that are in more exposed conditions have become weak and are being attacked by disease. We still do not have a replacement species that meets both aesthetic and durability requirements.

In conclusion the Air Force Academy was intended from the beginning to be an icon of the nation's building skills as well as an icon of architecture and modernism. Today it is up to the Air Force and interested groups to ensure that the Academy remains a remarkable example of its time. Those of us who are now stewards of its physical heritage are only beginning to understand the landscape. Today's challenge is to respond to growing pressure from development of the front range that threatens the viewsheds. A landscape infrastructure that is as important to the Academy as its architecture is being rebuilt. It is a task that must be dealt with in innovative ways and one that must be constantly publicized by people who understand that landscape architecture is not just planting trees and bushes but has its own rationale, theory, and aesthetics. It will be interesting to see how well a public bureaucracy deals with maintaining the vast holdings of open space and rebuilding a significant modern landscape that contribute to a growing, albeit not entirely established, heritage.

Duane Boyle, AIA, is Command Architect, United States Air Force Academy, Colorado Springs, Colorado.

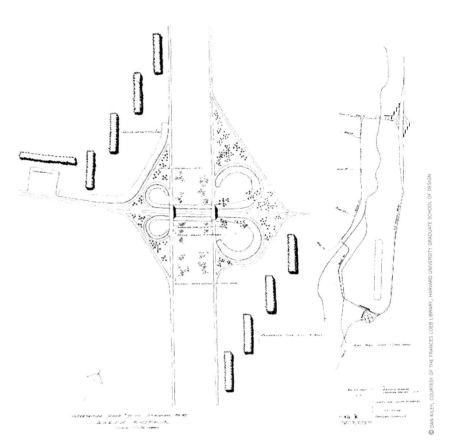

The staggered hedge used at the Miller Garden is considered in a sketch by Kiley's office for a freeway interchange at the Academy, 1957.

© DAN KILEY, COURTESY OF THE FRANCES LOEB LIBRARY, HARVARD UNIVERSITY GRADUATE SCHOOL OF DESIGN

36

The Air Garden at night, Air Force Academy, Colorado Springs, Colorado, c. 1958
Dan Kiley landscape architect. Photograph by Stewart's No. 38-27

Right: The Gateway Arch, St. Louis, Missouri, 1948-1976. Dan Kiley landscape
architect, Eero Saarinen architect. Photograph by Charles Birnbaum

The Miller Garden, Columbus, Indiana, 1955, original redbuds in adult garden, later replanted with crabapples. Dan Kiley landscape architect, Eero Saarinen architect. Photograph by Alan Ward.

Gainesway Farms, Lexington, Kentucky. A.E. Bye landscape architect. Photograph by A.E. Bye

Top: Hedgerow cluster, Sea Ranch, Gualala, Mendocino County, California. Master plan by Lawrence Halprin and Associates
Bottom: Lovejoy Fountain, Portland, Oregon. Photographs by Elizabeth K. Meyer

Top: Gas Works Park, Seattle Washington. Richard Haag landscape architect   Bottom: Bloedel Reserve, Bainbridge Island, Washington, Thomas Church, and later, Richard Haag landscape architects. Photographs by Elizabeth K. Meyer

42

Pepsico World Headquarters, Purchase, New York. Edward D. Stone, Jr., landscape architect. Pools by Russell Page, landscape gardener. Photograph by Peter Walker

Connecticut General Insurance Company (CIGNA) Headquarters, Hartford, Connecticut.
Courtyards designed by Isamu Noguchi. Photograph by David Walker

44

Ruth Bancroft Garden, Walnut Creek, California. Photograph by Mick Hales, courtesy of the Garden Conservancy

The Donnell Garden, Sonoma County, California. Thomas Church landscape architect. Photograph by Saxon Holt

The James Rose residence, today known as the James Rose Center in Ridgewood, New Jersey

Lincoln Center New York City. Dan Kiley landscape architect. Photograph Office of Dan Kiley.

Play panels 1967, Adventure Playground, New York City. Richard Dattner architect

Model by Isamu Noguchi for the Levy Memorial Playground, New York City, designed
with Louis I. Kahn. Photograph: Museum of Modern Art

The Challenge of Preserving Lincoln Center for the Performing Arts

Ken Smith

Dan Kiley's work at Lincoln Center must be considered in a broader context of mid-century modern landscape design projects. This context includes, in part, the work of Robert Zion at Paley Park and IBM Bamboo Garden; M. Paul Friedberg at Jacob Riis Park, and of Kiley himself at Lincoln Center, Rockefeller University, and the Ford Foundation. The contributions of these designers have been overlooked, especially those aspects of their work that addressed issues of livability and the renewal of urban centers in the postwar period.

Kiley, Zion, and Friedberg made significant contributions toward the development of a distinctive modern landscape architecture design vocabulary. As they encountered new building programs, changing social and cultural concerns, and advanced construction materials and technologies they sought contemporary design solutions and forms that reflected these new realities. Their design work is an expression of prevailing artistic ideas of the period—including the influences of cubism, constructivism, and minimalism. In historical context their works represent a dramatic departure from the romanticism of the English landscape tradition and the naturalism of Frederick Law Olmsted.

As a body of professional works these projects reflect mid-twentieth century concerns for renewing inner-city areas and creating landscaped open spaces that humanize the urban environment. The designers sought social and cultural responses to changing economic conditions of the postwar period, including the rise of a managerial work force, suburban commuting, and an increase in leisure time. Finally, their work reflected a new scale of urban renewal—superblock development—and pioneering construction technology that enabled the creation of landscapes on, in, and around structures.

After the 1970s the work of these designers was caught up in the architectural and social criticism of modernism in general and specifically of the anti-contextuality of mid-century urban-renewal projects. Thus, the significance of these seminal modern landscapes has been overlooked or dismissed because of changing social concerns and the counter movement of postmodernism.

Reevaluation is necessary if many of these seminal mid-century landscapes are to be saved from demolition, modification, and the damage caused by poor maintenance. The landscape designed by Kiley at Lincoln Center is a clear illustration of this. During the last fifteen years it has undergone a series of alterations resulting in the loss of a portion of the original design and a diminishment of other areas of the landscape. The remaining landscape—including Damrosch Park—is now undergoing assessment in preparation for future restoration efforts.

Very soon we will be speaking of the twentieth century in the past tense. Yet when we speak of historic preservation in landscape architecture we most often hear reference to works of the nineteenth century, including those of Frederick Law Olmsted, Sr., and of such founders of the American profession as Samuel Parsons, Jr., and Beatrix Jones Farrand. At best our profession's sense of history extends to include the estate period of the early twentieth century, encompassing possibly the public works of the 1930s, and occasionally the work of a few distinctive individuals such as Jens Jensen. It is time to expand the discussion of historic preservation in landscape architecture beyond the nineteenth century to include the landscapes of this century and in particular to recognize modernism as a social and cultural movement that produced a distinctive body of significant designed works.

In addressing the significance of twentieth-century landscape architecture we must acknowledge several factors that have contributed to its lack of recognition. Foremost is the problem of the invisibility of landscape as a design form. Works of landscape architecture often blend into and become part of the environment, invisible to most observers and known only to those whose scholarship or interest has led them to these places.

The second fundamental problem in preserving modern landscape architecture is the lack of well-documented histories. Unlike the profession of architecture—which has a more highly developed critical, theoretical, and historical underpinning—landscape architecture lacks the depth and ongoing research in the documentation of its own historical development. For too long the slender Museum of Modern Art overview *Modern Gardens and the Landscape* by Elizabeth Kassler served as the primary published history of the period. The past decade, to be sure, has seen major contributions to the documentation, analysis, and criticism of twentieth-century landscape architecture, but much more is needed to give the profession stronger theoretical underpinnings and documented critical history.

The third problem in preserving modern landscape architecture is a general antipathy toward modernism in the landscape. Modernism was never as widely embraced in the landscape as it was in architecture and other arts. Initially modernism was felt to be irrelevant because of landscape's separation from industrial process and material. Later, modernism was seen as contrary to the ecological, communitarian, and social concerns of the profession.

The fourth problem, which modern landscape architecture shares with landscape design of other historic periods, is the process of decline. The decline of landscape materials over time, especially such modern materials as concrete, plastics, and metals, makes these designed landscapes vulnerable to alteration and destruction at the very moment that the generational cycle of style or fashion holds the work at its lowest esteem. This, coupled with the lack of patronage in this country, often leaves the modern designed landscape without defenders. Decline is further exacerbated by neglect. Public works, in particular, are vulnerable because of the common public-policy mentality that favors one-time capital expenditures over ongoing operational and maintenance funding.

It is in this context that I will address the preservation of Kiley's designed landscape work at Lincoln Center for the Performing Arts in New York City. The landscape at Lincoln Center consists of several constituent parts that together create a unified designed landscape. While Kiley did not act as the landscape architect of record for all components of the landscape design, his involvement is clear, and the resulting design bears the trademarks of his design sensibility and practice.

At Lincoln Center Kiley designed planters with tightly spaced tree bosquets to create and manipulate landscape space, his design giving a sense of order and continuity to the complex as a whole. His use of strong, simple, and well-proportioned planters and plantings created spatial containment and a balanced relationship between a series of open plazas and courts and shaded bosquet areas. "Quartets" of plane trees were planted in twenty-foot-square travertine marble planters, which were partially recessed to minimize their scale. Kiley wrote that the crucial decision to include four trees in each planter was "essential to achieve the necessary mass and density for the plaza" and "to relate successfully to the surrounding architecture."[1] The serial layout of the planters with their "quartet" plantings created a distinctive spatial structure that defined a set of subordinate spaces. In the North Court the plane trees framed a reflecting pool and sculptures by Henry Moore and Alexander Calder. In Damrosch Park plane trees framed a sitting area set in a bosquet of purple leaf maples, and the perimeter of the band shell was framed with crabapples.

Kiley became involved as a member of the design team for Lincoln Center in the early 1960s. He was originally brought on as a collaborator with Eero Saarinen for work on the North Court in front of Beaumont Theater. In time his role expanded to that of primary designer for the landscape of Lincoln Center as a whole. "I worked very closely with all the Lincoln Center architects—Eero Saarinen, Pietro Belluschi, Gordon Bunshaft of SOM, Philip Johnson, Max Abramovitz, and Wally Harrison. All gave enthusiastic and unanimous approval to the final design," Kiley reports, "as did John D. Rockefeller III, so much so that Richard Webel, who had been assigned the design of Damrosch Park, was directed to incorporate precepts of my plan to assure site continuity."[2] Damrosch Park was to be part of the New York City Department of Parks and Recreation, which had hired landscape architect Richard Webel's firm, Darling, Innocenti & Webel (DI&W), to design the park. Kiley was commissioned by the design team for the design of other parts of Lincoln Center. An early design proposal for Damrosch Park by landscape architect Richard Webel shows a traditional park scheme, quite unlike the final Kiley design. In spite of the involvement of Webel's firm the design for all parts of the landscape at Lincoln Center bear the unmistakable influence of Kiley's involvement and his distinctive design approach.

Project correspondence, dated April 1, 1960, sheds some light on Kiley's role as designer relative to DI&W. While Kiley's office was involved in studying such major design issues as plaza drainage patterns; tree and ground-cover schedules; and planter seating, and fountain design, DI&W were directed to study peripheral items such as the location of a memorial flagpole and a possible sculpture panel. Further notes from the same correspondence reinforce the fact of Kiley's control of landscape-design issues. In one instance the Parks Department insisted on backrests for the seat walls that form the tree planters, and correspondence records that "it was generally agreed that a low plant box with both sides forming the required backrests would be an acceptable compromise between DI&W's proposals and those of Dan Kiley." The minutes conclude, "Dan Kiley will submit a design for future discussion."[3] And of course, in the as-built version of Damrosch Park there are no backrests, in keeping with Kiley's modern ideas and design intentions.

The design of plantings at Lincoln Center was complicated because the entire landscape was located over underground parking. Kiley was involved in critical issues of plantings, including precautions to "ensure tree life," with consideration given to proper drainage and protection from paved-area run-off contamination. Correspondence addresses the issue of soil depth and drainage in detail: "Minimum topsoil depth should be 36" in all beds plus 3" to 4" crushed stone at bottom and a 3" to 4" reveal at top to prevent washing and splashing of soil in rain." The planting palette, sizes, weights, and costs are discussed in detail in June 8, 1960, correspondence from the Office of Dan Kiley. By March 1961 the garage—located under the Lincoln Center landscape—was out for bid, and correspondence from the Office of Dan Kiley was inquiring about time schedules for installation and discussing planting selection and root-pruning requirements.[4]

The landscape at Lincoln Center

Maintenance and quality control were concerns from the beginning of the project. Much of the plant material for the project came from the Parks Department nursery at Riker's Island. Correspondence from September 16, 1963, through June 15, 1964, from Henry Arnold, who was working on the project for the Office of Dan Kiley, indicates many plants were rejected for poor quality or bad physical form. "The Ginkgo trees that were recently planted are not good specimens. In such an important area these trees should be perfectly formed specimens in addition to meeting caliper and height specifications. Dan was very disappointed with the trees that were used." Arnold continues, "Someone has planted miscellaneous types of shrubs and flowers under the Sargent crabapple trees in the planter along the front. These planters can be filled with red geraniums, and in the fall chrysanthemums, to make a broad band of color under the crabapple trees until they fill in. The plants that have been scattered there now only detract from the appearance. We hope that this can be remedied soon."[5]

In addition to concerns about the quality of landscape materials being installed correspondence also expresses concern about the maintenance of landscape installations. Kiley writes to Max Abramovitz: "In passing the Lincoln Center site the other day, I took a look at the plane trees in the boxes in front of Eero's building. It would benefit these trees very much both for their strength and also for the final form we wish to maintain, to clip the tops back to form a horizontal surface. I hope you realize the importance of my following up on the details of this planting in order to insure the results we intended."[6] Kiley's letter was forwarded by Harrison & Abramovitz to the Department of Parks and Recreation, but the recommendation was not followed.

By the middle to late 1980s the landscape at Lincoln Center, including Damrosch Park and the North Court, had matured. Photographs taken by the author in 1988 show the park and landscape areas in apparent health and vigor. The mature park was beautiful and well used. At this time plans were developed for the restoration of the roof membrane under the North Court area of the Lincoln Center landscape, and Kiley was not consulted when plans were developed for the alteration of the design for this area. Horticulturists who did not recognize the historic significance of the design and believed the design to be flawed fundamentally altered and diminished the character and strength of this area of the project. Kiley's original quartet plantings of plane trees were replaced by single plantings of ornamental pears, and his unified ground cover of flowering Japanese azaleas was replaced with old-fashioned bedding plants. Photographs taken before and after project work illustrate just how much was lost in terms of the integrity of the original design.

North Court, 1988

North Court, 1995

A further erosion of Lincoln Center's other landscape spaces began soon after with removal of trees from the Damrosch Park and band-shell areas. Contributing to the loss of design integrity in these areas have been serious issues of tree health and maintenance. Operational concerns relative to disease and the maturity of the original plant material have been addressed with a program of disease control, pruning, and root feeding. However, as the landscape grows beyond the thirty-year mark it is expected that disease and maturity will continue to take their toll.

In 1993 architect Robert A.M. Stern wrote to Lincoln Center out of concern over the changes that were occurring to the landscape. He stated that "while the value of preserving beautiful and historic buildings is widely recognized, the same recognition and protection are not yet often afforded to landscape design. Though they are by no means static, the best works of landscape design are indeed works of art that should be carefully preserved. The materials the landscape designer has chosen, including particular trees and shrubs, as well as their placement, must be respected."[7]

In 1995 a small group of concerned landscape architects and architects formed a committee to press the issue of preserving Kiley's design for the landscape at Lincoln Center and to press for a historic preservation approach to Damrosch Park, the North Court, and associated designed landscape areas. In September 1995 representatives of the committee met with the management of Lincoln Center to discuss the future of Kiley's design work at Lincoln Center, and Lincoln Center has begun to replace plant materials in Damrosch Park in keeping with the original design. Restoration efforts are needed for the band-shell area and Kiley's North Court to reverse previous alterations. While there is much work to be done in terms of raising funds and preparing plans for future restoration, Lincoln Center's commitment to recognizing the importance of Kiley's design and to restoring the project in a historically sensitive and responsible manner is to be commended.

As one of the nation's premier arts institutions Lincoln Center is on the verge of embarking on what promises to be a leadership role in the preservation of modern landscapes. Lincoln Center—with the involvement of Kiley and other advisors on modern landscape design, historic landscape preservation, and urban arboriculture—is beginning a process to determine a prudent course of action for the future maintenance and restoration of this nationally significant designed landscape.

The preservation of Kiley's work at Lincoln Center illustrates the problems of preserving modern landscape architecture. First, the alterations to Kiley's work at Lincoln Center resulted not from a malicious attempt to destroy this important designed landscape, but from the lack of knowledge of its historical significance. As the profession of landscape architecture moves to better assess and document its history—especially its recent history—practitioners and citizens will be better informed so that they may intervene to protect significant designed landscapes. Second, the late 1980s alterations to the North Court landscape occurred at a time when architectural fashion championed a decorative postmodernist aesthetic and the appreciation of modern landscape design was at its nadir. The lesson, perhaps, is to resist the passions of current fashion. Third, the landscape at Lincoln Center illustrates the problems of a lack of consistent funding for the maintenance of landscape design.

The final lesson is the importance of having a committed body of professionals who are knowledgeable about landscape-design history and willing to become active in preserving and maintaining built works of modern landscape architecture. If it were not for the commitment of the landscape architecture and architecture community we would not be considering the preservation of the landscape at Lincoln Center and many other equally important designed landscapes from the modern era.

Ken Smith is a landscape architect in New York City, New York.

1 The author wishes to express his gratitude to Dan Kiley for making copies of his project correspondence available. Letter from Dan Kiley to Robert A.M. Stern, October 20, 1993.

2 Ibid.

3 Meeting minutes of March 31, 1960, project meeting at the office of architects Harrison & Abramovitz, April 1, 1960.

4 Correspondence from the Office of Dan Kiley to Harrison & Abramovitz, May 24, 1960, and project minutes.

5 Correspondence from Henry Arnold, Office of Dan Kiley, to Max Abramovitz, May 19, 1964. (Further correspondence from Henry Arnold, June 24, 1964, gives a detailed listing of unacceptable plantings.)

6 Correspondence from Kiley to Abramovitz, August 23, 1965. On September 15, 1966, Henry Arnold of the Office of Dan Kiley writes Harrison & Abramovitz to note that a "large number" of azaleas were dead and that they should be replaced "regularly as part of the maintenance program." Correspondence from Harrison & Abramovitz on October 4, 1966, indicates correction of remaining items on the construction punch list and acceptance of the work by the Department of Parks and Recreation. This letter, addressed to the Director of Engineering at the Parks and Recreation Department, closes with specific recommendations regarding the maintenance of the project landscape: "All landscaped areas require adequate care and maintenance. We suggest that a regular schedule be put into operation by the Department of Parks."

7 Letter from Robert A.M. Stern to Nathan Leventhal, president of Lincoln Center for the Performing Arts, September 8, 1993.

52

Playing for Time:
Preservation Issues in
Contemporary Playground Design
Lisa E. Crowder

The Playground Movement in the United States dates back to the turn of the twentieth century, a time when urban populations were exploding and the social ills exacerbated by this growth provided the catalyst for many social movements. One of the most significant of these was Progressivism, the proponents of which were responsible for many reforms directed toward the welfare of children, including the creation of kindergartens, nursery schools, and playgrounds.[1] One Progressive idea was to increase the efficiency of society through streamlining and standardizing the various component parts of which it was made. Progressivists considered the playground to be a vital tool for the reform of childhood. Playgrounds provided an institutional framework for ensuring social conformity of children, particularly immigrant children. The regimentation of play was meant to transform the personality of each individual child into one "perfectly suited to meet the stresses and challenges of twentieth-century urban-industrial society."[2]

During this era American playgrounds took on a form that has largely remained unchanged to this day, providing open areas for team sports for older children and smaller areas of equipment and sand for younger children. One of the instruments for the standardization of American playgrounds was the Playground Association of America, formed in 1906. It identified the social ends of play as "cleanliness, politeness, formation of friendships, obedience to law, loyalty, justice, honesty, truthfulness, and determination."[3]

Few landscape architects participated in the Playground Movement in a significant way. Designers generally perceived playgrounds as a necessary evil, the unaesthetic and disruptive nature of which they saw as inherent in the playground's function. In 1920 Frederick Law Olmsted, Jr., made clear the prevailing philosophy of the profession regarding playgrounds when he wrote, "On the whole . . . the necessary ingredients of a city playground do not tend to make it beautiful perforce, any more than a railroad bridge or a highway bridge is beautiful perforce." Like his father before him Olmsted considered that the "one sound justification of large parks is a purely esthetic one, [and] if they are to be justified at all it is only by adhering steadfastly to this purpose as the controlling one in all decisions effecting their design and management."[4] He suggested, therefore, that playgrounds be distinctly separated from park land in order to avoid detracting from the public enjoyment. Since the focus of landscape architects was generally on projects of a grander scale, the design of the vast majority of playgrounds fell to park or school administrators, for whom ease of maintenance was frequently the most important consideration.

Contemporary playground design can be divided into five overlapping phases. The artist period dates back to the 1930s with the unrealized designs of Isamu Noguchi. *Play Mountain* (1933) was Noguchi's first attempt to mold the earth into shapes appropriate for play (Figure 1). Noguchi considered his playgrounds "primers of shapes and functions; simple, mysterious, and evocative: thus, educational."[5] This period reached its zenith in the 1950s and 1960s, when such institutions as the Museum of Modern Art and the Corcoran Gallery sponsored competitions to design play equipment. These competitions frequently produced models of abstract pieces of play equipment, although few were ever installed. A few notable exceptions, such as the Alice in Wonderland group in Central Park with an associated landscape designed by Hideo Sasaki, were successful additions to the urban landscape.

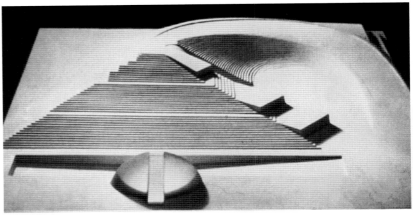

Figure 1. Model of Play Mountain, *Isamu Noguchi, 1933*

The 1950s and 1960s also produced a more lasting phase in the history of playground design, the novelty equipment period. Responding to growing concerns over safety and child-development issues, play equipment manufacturers began to employ new media in the creation of fantasy-oriented equipment. One of the goals of this period was to encourage imaginative play by reshaping traditional equipment in novel forms. Manufacturers used concrete, fiberglass, and plastic to create animals, vehicles (both realistic and futuristic), and abstract shapes.

The environmental period in American playground design was a direct response to the European adventure-playground movement. Adventure playgrounds appeared following World War II and represented a completely new paradigm for play. Vacant lots were fenced off and filled with junk (old tires, wood, nails, rope, bricks) that children, under the supervision of an experienced play leader, were free to manipulate as they chose. Whereas the historical focus of the American playground has been the physical aspects of play, the adventure playground provides an environment that fosters the multiple aspects of child development. However, adventure playgrounds never achieved popularity in the United States. Even more than traditional playgrounds they are noisy, messy, and thoroughly unattractive, and Americans generally perceive them as inherently dangerous.

Although many designers in America espouse the adventure-playground ethic, few have actually designed playgrounds that resemble European adventure playgrounds. The most notable exceptions, such as Clare Cooper Marcus and Robin Moore, are European. Two notable American designers who credit the adventure-playground movement with providing the philosophical foundation for their own work are M. Paul Friedberg and Richard Dattner. They are probably the two most visible leaders of the next phase of playground design, the designer phase.

In *Play and Interplay* (1970) Friedberg proposed the concept of "linked" play, in which the play experience continues between and among the various elements. As he put it, "a child can climb up and down, go through a variety of experiences on any mound, and enjoy moving from one mound to the next."[6] Friedberg was also a pioneer of modular play equipment. His modular wooden play structures are a progenitor of the manufactured landscape structures that currently dominate the design of playgrounds. He originally proposed that the modules—created of pressure-treated wood timbers—be constructed so that the children could combine and recombine them, thus allowing for a certain degree of dynamism in the environment. However, the do-it-yourself play environments that sprang up across the country, were essentially static assemblages of play equipment executed in steel rather than wood.

Dattner's playgrounds represent a synthesis of the adventure playground, Noguchi's landforms, and traditional playground design. His Adventure Playground in Central Park bears little resemblance to a European adventure playground. Dattner's Adventure Playground was a sanitized, aestheticized version of the European model and with its mounds, steps, walls, slides, and tunnels was clearly reminiscent of Noguchi's playground designs. Dattner's style remained consistent through this period, providing architectonic mound forms, surrounded by sweeps of sand and accompanied by aesthetically improved versions of traditional play equipment. Like Friedberg, Dattner made judicious use of wooden structures in some playgrounds—although concrete was his primary medium.

Designer playgrounds frequently incorporated water, either through the inclusion of wading pools, sprays, fountains, or waterfalls. Few of these water features remain operational. Liability and maintenance issues generally are responsible for the disuse of these features. Indeed, liability issues in general led to the demise of the designer era, setting the stage for the current phase in playground design, most suitably known as the high-tech equipment era. High-tech equipment represents a fusion of traditional play equipment with the modular forms popularized by Friedberg and others.

Once again, equipment manufacturers have taken the lead, responding, as they did during the novelty era, to concerns about safety and child-development issues. Design improvements, coupled with technological advances, have created safer versions of playground equipment with jazzier colors and more bells and whistles. Playground superstructures that accommodate five children or five hundred can be ordered and installed on-site with liability insurance provided by most manufacturers. Generally speaking, current playgrounds for which landscape architects receive design credit are customized versions of these catalog playgrounds. Possibly the best of these customized playgrounds, and probably the best known, is the playground at Hudson River Park in Battery Park City, a product of the Johansson and Walcavage firm. This design shows greater sensitivity to the ultimate client—the children—than do most playground installations. High-tech designs as a class, however, show how little the playground design tradition has evolved in the past hundred years.

Restoration Issues and Contemporary Playground Design

Now we turn to the preservation issues confronting works of contemporary playground design. Many of these problems—such as wear and tear, graffiti and vandalism, and public perception of the landscape as unsafe, unaesthetic, or outdated—are common to most urban landscapes. Another problem shared by many historic landscapes is the general pressure to make the highest and best use, in other words the most profitable use, of all urban land. This frequently results in development that encroaches on park lands or lands where development was previously perceived as prohibitively expensive—sites where playgrounds are often located. Trying to ward off encroachment on environmental playgrounds is even more difficult because they are not perceived as useful landscapes. Everyone knows what a playground looks like, and the environmental playground does not fit the bill. The administrators of playgrounds are also likely to pose a problem. Public parks departments may possess the technical skill necessary to maintain a historic landscape but generally are lacking in design expertise or an understanding of child development. School administrators may understand the child-development issues related to playgrounds, but they lack technical or design skills as well as money and time to deal with such an esoteric

Figure 2. New York City neighborhood playground with equipment typical of the novelty equipment era of the 1950s and 1960s

concern. Each of these issues may pose problems for the preservation of playgrounds. By far the most important issues in this regard, however, are those relating to safety and child development.

Figures from the Consumer Products Safety Commission (CPSC) indicate that approximately 170,000 children receive treatment in hospital emergency rooms each year for injuries related to the use of playground equipment. Public playgrounds, either in parks or school yards, account for roughly seventy percent of this number. In response to safety concerns the CPSC has released two handbooks for public playground safety, the first in 1981 and a second in 1991. In December 1993 the American Society for Testing and Materials released the first national standards for playground equipment, and in 1986 a national survey of community-park playground equipment was undertaken by the Committee on Play of the American Association for Leisure and Recreation. One of the conclusions of the study was that "America's community playgrounds are not safe."[7] The study notes that "extensive retrofits of existing playground structures with excessive heights and hard undersurfaces simply must take place. Today's generation of children are clearly at physical risk from these high structures and hazardous installations."[8] The most common cause of serious injury or fatality on playgrounds is a fall to a hard surface, and "climbers, slides, and swings were the most frequently reported types of injury-related equipment."[9] Other common hazards include: entanglement of clothing on protruding bolts; head/neck entrapment; hard swing seats/animal swings; improper or missing guardrails; improper rung sizes and spacing; improper fall zones and no-encroachment zones; insufficient distances from walls and fences; crush and shear points.[10]

These issues are basic to any playground preservation plan, as is the environment's child-development potential. As we have seen, there has been very little significant change in the design of children's playgrounds since the turn of the century even though development theory has made quantum leaps in the same time. Luther Gulick, one of the leaders of the Playground Movement, popularized the "recapitulation" theory of play, maintaining that, through play, a child repeats the stages of human evolution. This theory proposed an explanation for childhood activities such as digging, climbing trees, and playing with water. Since that time, play and its place in the development of a child have been the subject of extensive

PHOTOS: CHARLES A. BIRNBAUM

Figure 3. Rehabilitated Playscapes in Piedmont Park, Atlanta, Georgia, 1998

research. It is now generally accepted that play and exploration are central to the adaptability, learning, cognitive development, socioemotional development, and early education of young children.[11] Research also shows that the play and learning environment can significantly affect child development and education. Children exposed to a greater variety of stimulation generally show higher levels of cognitive, language, and memory development as well as attention to novelty. Most equipment-based playgrounds are, however, virtually indistinguishable from each other. They offer little variety or stimulation and are fundamentally static, sterile environments lacking in the dynamic qualities necessary for facilitating child development.

Isamu Noguchi's Playscapes, Atlanta, Georgia: A Case Study

Isamu Noguchi began proposing playground designs in the early 1930s. Both on his own and with collaborators he made proposals for numerous playgrounds. However, the only Noguchi playground ever implemented in the United States was his 1976 installation *Playscapes*, a gift from the High Museum of Art to the City of Atlanta on the occasion of the United States Bicentennial (Figure 3). In an unpublished teacher's guide in the Department of Children's Education, the High Museum described *Playscapes* as "an expression of [the museum's] goals and philosophy in working with children. . . . It is, first and last, a place where children enjoy themselves in 'a geometric confrontation with the world.'"

The playground is located in Piedmont Park in midtown Atlanta, only a few blocks from the High Museum. This park, designed by the Olmsted office, is the largest park in Atlanta and the site of festivals and other events throughout the year. Part of the original playground design includes a shelter and classroom with office and darkroom facilities. The High Museum used the playground for more than a decade as the setting for a successful summer art-awareness program for children. However, as is the case with many urban parks throughout the country, Piedmont Park suffers from considerable image problems. The majority of the population of Atlanta is suburban, and many consider the entire downtown area to be unsafe.

Perception problems alone were not responsible for the downfall of *Playscapes*. Changes in the administration of the High Museum, employee turnover, and new directions in the museum's educational-outreach programs also contributed to letting

Playscapes "fall through the cracks." By 1991 the museum was no longer holding its summer education sessions at the playground, and without the museum's involvement, the maintenance of *Playscapes* fell solely to the Atlanta Parks Department. Although *Playscapes* is intact and largely unchanged, it is in a sad state of neglect.

Under the direction of the Piedmont Park Conservancy, a nonprofit organization, *Playscapes* has been rehabilitated. The playground was rededicated on September 9, 1996, the twentieth anniversary of its opening. The $300,000 project was completed with the in-kind services of Kajima Construction Services, Inc., as well as the support of the Piedmont Park Conservancy, the High Museum of Art, the Isamu Noguchi Foundation, and the City of Atlanta. The work included the repair, repainting, and general restoration of the equipment, the renovation of the classroom structure, and other general restoration of the playground.

The Rehabilitation of *Playscapes*

Prior to this work a number of questions needed to be asked. First, is it safe? The staff of the Piedmont Park Conservancy is unaware of any safety audit of the playground, and this factor was not considered in the rehabilitation planning. Nevertheless, even a superficial look at the playground shows significant safety hazards. Most notably, these include inappropriate surfacing, dangerous heights, and safety-design flaws in equipment. The general perception of the park as unsafe has not changed significantly since the High abandoned it in 1991. The Conservancy considers safety problems to be primarily a "police and programming issue." Whether or not the playground can be made safe without compromising its integrity is uncertain. Although surfacing problems have been addressed, the safety of individual equipment pieces is suspect.

Is it developmentally appropriate for its intended users? Despite its noted designer *Playscapes* is not significantly different with regard to child-development issues from a playground filled with less rarefied equipment. Consequently, the experience is primarily static and lacks the dynamism necessary for a good play environment. However, since the site is not intended to serve as an "everyday" playground, but only for infrequent visits by children, its novelty and artistic aspects probably can be seen as providing appropriate developmental experiences for children in middle childhood.

Are the administration and funding in place to maintain the playground over the long term? This, too, is debatable. If the administration of the playground remains in the hands of the city parks department, it is doubtful that any rehabilitation project would have lasting effect. If administration of the playground is turned over to a nonprofit organization, such as the Piedmont Park Conservancy or the High Museum, its future would again depend on the whims of funding and the interest of individual staff members.

Is adequate supervision available? The playground is often loosely supervised when in use because many of the children who visit *Playscapes* are part of a group, either a class from one of the area schools or part of an extracurricular group. There is, however, no general system of supervision, nor is an official play leader provided for in the plan for the playground's rehabilitation.

Is the playground historically significant? This question alone can be answered with an unqualified "yes." As the only Noguchi playground ever constructed in the United States it holds a unique place in the history of landscape design.

Can the preservation of *Playscapes* be justified as a historic landscape regardless of possible safety defects and child-development concerns? This question lies at the heart of playground preservation. *Playscapes*, as a historic landscape, is undoubtedly significant, but real concerns about safety exist. Furthermore, although it is not developmentally inappropriate, it offers relatively little in this regard to recommend it over safer alternatives. Finally, given the potential that any rehabilitation attempt may ultimately meet the same fate as the original installation, are the expense and effort worthwhile or merely an exercise in futility?

It is not my intention to provide answers to these questions, but only to point out some of the challenges unique to the preservation of playgrounds. In conclusion, I will leave you with one final issue to consider. Given the vast changes that have occurred during the past century in our understanding of play and its place in child development and early childhood education, are "historically significant" playgrounds so hopelessly outdated and unsafe that their preservation poses a real threat to the intended users? If so, can we justify their preservation as functional landscapes? If we cannot, can their preservation be justified based solely on their place in the design tradition?

Lisa E. Crowder is an independent researcher and playground designer based in Decatur, Georgia.

1   Michael Stephen Shapiro, *Child's Garden: The Kindergarten Movement from Froebel to Dewey* (University Park, Pennsylvania: Pennsylvania State University Press, 1983).

2   Dominick Cavallo, *Muscles and Morals: Organized Playgrounds and Urban Reforms, 1880-1920* (Philadelphia: University of Pennsylvania Press, 1981), 11.

3   Joe L. Frost, *Play and Playscapes* (Albany: Delmar Publishers, 1992), 121.

4   Frederick Law Olmsted, Jr., "Parks and Playgrounds," *The Playground* (1920), 347-52.

5   Isamu Noguchi, *A Sculptor's World* (New York: Harper and Row, 1968), 161.

6   Paul Friedberg, *Play and Interplay* (New York: MacMillan, 1970), 44.

7   R. Smith, "Plan of Action: Reflections and Recommendations," *Where Our Children Play: Community Park Playground Equipment*, ed. Donna Thompson and Louis Bowers (Reston, Virginia: American Alliance for Health, Physical Education, Recreation, and Dance, 1989), 86.

8   M. Crawford, "Swings, Slides, and Climbing Equipment," *Where Our Children Play*, 47.

9   D.K. Tinsworth, "Public Playground Equipment-Related Injuries and Deaths," *Play It Safe: An Anthology of Playground Safety*, ed. C.L. Christiansen (Arlington, Virginia: National Recreation and Park Association, 1992), 66.

10 F. Wallach, "Playground Hazard Identification," *Play It Safe*, 125-26.

11 D.A. Caruso, "Play and Learning in Infancy: Research and Implications," *Young Children*, 63-70.

M. Paul Friedberg's Early Playground Designs in New York City

Alison Dalton

M. Paul Friedberg is internationally known for his many landscape and planning projects, but perhaps his greatest contributions to the field of landscape architecture have been his innovations in the realm of playground design. In the early 1960s, at a time when playgrounds consisted largely of fenced-off areas containing a few pieces of standard equipment (slide, swing, seesaw), Friedberg began a series of explorations that were to lead him to the concept of continuous play and to the design of the playground as an integrated part of an architectural whole. His playgrounds appeal to the adult eye as much as to the childhood imagination, reflecting his predilection for sculpted landscapes defined by dramatic grade changes and powerful geometrical forms unified by a strong sense of procession.

Friedberg's playground and urban-park projects of the 1960s and early 1970s also reflected the era in which they were conceived. Many politicians and planners, concerned about urban blight and optimistic about the possibilities of social renewal, were inspired by a sense of mission. John Lindsay was elected mayor of New York City in 1965. Also at this time Thomas Hoving, later, president of the Metropolitan Museum of Art, was made commissioner of the Department of Parks and Recreation. At the same time, socially minded private foundations such as the Astor Foundation, as well as the federal government, made funding available. These new brooms swept in a series of radically different urban and recreational-space projects that utilized some of the best landscape and architectural talents of the day, Paul Friedberg among them.

It has been said that Friedberg created the first adventure playground in New York. I would argue Friedberg's were not true adventure playgrounds in that they did not contain any movable parts; they were not manipulatable environments. In some ways they represented a middle ground between the adventure playground and the Moses playground, including the slides and swings if not the seesaws of the Moses era but placing them in a far more interesting and adventurous context.

Between 1967 and 1968 Friedberg designed a series of experimental "portable playgrounds" for the New York City Department of Parks. These were constructed of pipe-frame and concrete modules, wood timbers, and pipe-and-cable units that did not require foundations and were intended to be used in vacant lots in areas where there were few play facilities—such as in Bedford-Stuyvesant. The components could be erected cheaply and quickly and just as easily disassembled.[1] Unfortunately, funds for actually demounting and reassembling these playgrounds were always lacking, and the original concept of portability was lost.

At the Riverview, a housing project on 140th Street in Manhattan, Friedberg discovered the potential of land forms for play. While the site was under construction in 1970 children played happily on the many rock outcroppings and on the terraced steps that Friedberg installed to accommodate the natural grade. When novelty play equipment of the sort then enjoying a vogue—concrete spaceship and trees—was finally added to the playground, it almost proved a liability. The pieces were in conflict with the site and offered only static play experiences, while the rocks, the steps, and the concrete-bollard stepping platforms proved much more successful.[2]

The Mulberry Street Park was one of a series of ten "vest-pocket" parks

29th Street vest-pocket park

designed between 1967 and 1968. Friedberg envisioned a series of play places that would be linked to other community facilities and create a "living corridor" throughout the city. Vacant lots, alleyways, small parks, and the like could be transformed from ignored, leftover spaces to vital, usable, visually exciting places.[3] The vest-pocket parks allowed Friedberg to experiment with bold graphics and various modular play systems, including metal pipe and wood timbers, as he did at the Mulberry Street Park.

Another vest-pocket park, at Twenty-ninth Street and Second Avenue in Manhattan, was intended as a prototype for a whole series of city parks, each intended to focus on a different aspect of natural science. The play area's climbing mound was to cover a planetarium's dome. Unfortunately, the science-park projects were never realized.

In 1966 the Riis Housing Plaza in the Lower East Side brought Friedberg into prominence as a public open-space designer of vision. The plaza as it existed consisted of a series of concrete walks, bordered by benches and separated by fenced-off expanses of turf. Friedberg reconceived the plaza as a processional series of open spaces, rhythmically modulating height and depth, openness and enclosure to achieve a wonderfully varied and eminently usable public space. The procession begins with a semi-enclosed fountain area, continues to a large amphitheater (featuring a water channel and pool and a projecting stage), proceeds through a sitting and viewing area, and culminates with the playground.

Riis Housing Project

The playground has been described as "a miniature Egyptian landscape, complete with pyramids and sand."[4] It also contained a granite igloo with three side entrance tunnels and a ladder through the top, a wood-timber play area, an adjacent seating area, numerous pieces of integrated metal climbing equipment, tree houses, and a concrete maze. In the Riis playground Friedberg fully realized his concept of linked play: Getting from one piece of play equipment to another became part of the play experience itself. The movement down one granite mound would carry the child up the next. Physical links included planks, cable, and ropes. Children were able to create their own play patterns and were not stuck in a designer-prescribed play loop.

Soon after, in late 1966, Friedberg was given the opportunity to design the open spaces of the Bedford-Stuyvesant superblock with I.M. Pei. The central concept of the superblock was that cars, then parked on either side of the street, would now be parked in the center. This would leave ample room for recreational and passive areas on the sides and in the central interstices. The play area was visually and spatially integrated with the rest of the project, partially through the use of graphics.

The P.S. 166 Playground of 1967 on West Eighty-ninth Street in Manhattan shows what Friedberg had learned in his previous work. Sunk three feet below grade for a sense of containment, it held a number of geometrized granite-block landforms—a mountain and canyons or caves—and an imaginative variety of playlinks, including springboards, bridges, fireman's poles, cables, and ladders. The climbing mound concealed lavatories. Trees were planted throughout the play area, including on top of a mound. There were a tree house, a "spider's web" of cables suspended between posts, and an amphitheater with spray fountains.[5]

The nearby Gottesman Plaza Playground of 1970 on West Ninety-fourth Street was an object lesson in the necessity of considering future maintenance as part of a playground's design. The plaza contained a ball court, a seating area, and a play area containing a granite pyramid and graphics-ornamented metal-pipe play equipment. Unfortunately the playground was soon vandalized due to inadequate supervision and poor maintenance.[6] The Gottesman has been demolished and exists only as several heaps of rubble.

In fact, very little remains of Friedberg's seminal playground work. The vest-pocket parks and the portable playgrounds have disappeared. The Twenty-ninth Street park has been altered beyond recognition. Riis Plaza playground and the P.S. 166 Playground, the two best examples of his work, still exist—but in a state of decay. At Riis the sand surface has disappeared, the igloo tunnels have been closed up, the tree houses and the metal climbing equipment are gone. The timber play forms have been vandalized, the wood steps are decayed, and some granite blocks are missing. It is interesting to note that even with many of its original features missing the playground still works: It has great "bones."

The P.S. 166 Playground was threatened with destruction. And, indeed, it has suffered losses over the years. The water play no longer functions; metal climbers are missing as are granite blocks; the lavatories have been closed off; the banners, the tree house, the springboards, and the spider's web are gone. Simple lack of maintenance has created unsafe conditions. In 1996 and 1997 community members, school officials, and preservationists rallied to save the playground. After intense negotiations it was determined that it could not be saved because it did not meet current safety codes. As a result of these negotiations Friedberg was brought back to design a new playground in the spirit of the original—complete with amphitheater. This project has achieved consensus and will be completed in 2000.

The loss and potential loss of Friedberg's works raise troubling questions for landscape architects today. We have largely relegated playground design to equipment manufacturers and ignored the loss of irreplaceable play landscapes to the detriment of both our profession and the public. True, in playgrounds the preservation issues that confront us in other landscapes are further complicated by safety issues: Hospital statistics tell us that playgrounds are unsafe environments for children, and the almost universally accepted Consumer Products Safety Commission and American Society for Testing and Materials safety codes do dictate a circumscribed set of design standards.

Does this mean that significant playgrounds that require rehabilitation or reconstruction due to their age must be altered beyond recognition and stripped of the very features that make them both historical and memorable? We have an opportunity at P.S. 166 and at other important play areas to chart a course for future playground preservation. We can examine them on a case by case basis, determining how "dangerous" individual playscapes truly are. The P.S.166 Playground has never, in almost thirty years of continuous use, experienced a serious accident. This is compelling evidence that a complete redesign on the grounds of safety may be unnecessary. Moreover, intelligent retrofitting of playgrounds can be done. For instance, at P.S. 166 more hand- and foot-holds could be installed in the granite climbing mounds, and railings placed at their tops.

Drawing for P.S.166 Playground, New York City

More and better safety surfaces could be installed, and climbing equipment moved away from hard surfaces.

We must also begin to consider planned maintenance as a design issue and as something that must, whenever possible, be negotiated in the design process. Nothing contributes to a landscape's demise faster than the lack of proper maintenance and supervision, as seen at Gottesman Plaza.

Friedberg sought inspiration for urban playground form and experience in nature itself. His granite-block pyramids and bowls are geometrized rock formations that are begging to be climbed and explored; his sand play surfaces reference the sand beach of the shore or desert dunes; his spray fountains are a city kid's stream. These designs were of vast importance in changing the way we conceived of and designed for play; today the very few that remain are some of the most compelling of our urban spaces. They cry out for preservation.

A few words about the future of playground design: Friedberg's central tenet of continuous play gave children the opportunity to create their own play patterns, but those patterns were chiefly those of body, not mind. Today, thanks to advances in childhood-development studies, we know that children need far more than physical exercise: They need dramatic play; they need to create their own games and structures; they need to interact and negotiate their play experience with other children. In the words of R.D. Laing, "the two most important human needs are experience, and control over one's experience."

Our era's dispiriting return to a 1950s play mentality—stock equipment on a safety surface—is perhaps balanced by new forays into playground design. Some designers envision contained natural ecosystems as play areas. Others are taking a new look at the adventure playground, in which children have an opportunity to manipulate their environment. This last category includes, interestingly, Friedberg himself. His new playground project in San Francisco includes giant Styrofoam building blocks, sound tubes, sand areas with water that comes from beneath the sand surface, solar- and wind-powered devices, and other items that allow children to indulge their innate curiosity about the world and natural forces that surround them. Such features as a giant chalk wall invite creative expression. For, in Friedberg's words, "the single most exciting piece of equipment on a playground is a piece of chalk."

Alison Dalton is a landscape designer in New York, New York.

1 "Lincoln Logs," *Architectural Forum* (April 1966), 82.

2 Paul Friedberg, conversation with the author, October 9, 1995, New York City.

3 "Urban Playscapist," *Progressive Architecture* (August 1966), 70-72.

4 Jonathan Barnett, Foreword, "Paul Friedberg's Contribution to Landscape Design," *Process Architecture* (May 1989).

5 "Designing the Spaces In Between," *Architectural Record* (March 1968), 121-32.

6 Paul Friedberg, conversation with the author, October 9, 1995, New York City.

The Politics of Play:
The Adventure Playground in Central Park
Michael Gotkin

Introduction

Central Park was declared a New York City Scenic Landmark in 1975 and recognized as a New York State Historic Site in 1978; it has been listed in the National Register of Historic Places since 1972. That the sylvan landscape composition is worthy of mandated protection and preservation is without question. Great controversy has, however, arisen regarding the sanctity of the innumerable components that comprise Central Park, including paths, benches, buildings, sculpture, fountains, zoos, and recreational facilities. Amenities that were added to the park in the twentieth century—particularly those features that have attempted to assert design principles resonant with their own time—are especially vulnerable to modification and removal at the hands of park preservationists. Playgrounds are an apt example of design features that have become integral—both spatially and experientially—to Central Park but are lacking the protection of city, state, and federal landmarks laws. Although the history of children's outdoor play is intimately tied to the history of Central Park and even though the concept of children's play was a design consideration of the park's founding sponsors and landscape architects, this aspect of the park's historic landscape design has been significantly compromised in recent years.[1] The rich store of innovative designs for children's play contained within Central Park includes one of the most important and influential playgrounds in America: the Adventure Playground, designed by architect Richard Dattner in 1966. Today, the Adventure Playground of Central Park provides a remarkable example of a notable modern design within the historic park that has engendered great controversy over its preservation and restoration. The story of this playground and the battle to preserve it illustrates the interface of politics, ideology, and design in planning New York City's designed landscapes—a tale of great interest to those concerned with the preservation of modern landscape architecture.

Central Park and Modern Landscape Design

Although the pastoral scenery of Central Park and the precepts of modernism may appear to be diametrically opposed, the park actually contains numerous and significant examples of modern landscape design. The generally accepted historical image of Central Park is of a mid-nineteenth-century landscape design conceived and executed by landscape architects Frederick Law Olmsted, Sr., and Calvert Vaux. This interpretation, however, ignores the significant contribution and vision of several key individuals involved with the creation of the park and dismisses subsequent additions and modifications to the park landscape over time. Even the original Olmsted and Vaux design was modified several times during two decades of construction. Changes and additions to the park continued after the withdrawal of Frederick Law Olmsted, Sr., under the stewardship of Calvert Vaux and his successors, including such notable landscape architects as Samuel Parsons, Jr., and Gilmore D. Clarke. Because of the great number of significant contributors and contributions to the Central Park landscape over time it is not practicable, nor even desirable, to document a specific period of significance for the park. Central Park is not, and has never been, a consistent architectonic conception, but rather, like the city that surrounds it, a variegated composition that displays the contributions of myriad designers, citizens, politicians, and historical epochs. It is precisely this great richness of diversity that characterizes both city and park.

The dominant vision for Central Park is certainly the collective design by Olmsted and Vaux and several of their less famous collaborators (for example, chief gardener Ignaz Pilat and park commissioners Andrew Green and Waldo Hutchins); however, this seminal vision is actually a framework or superstructure within which are contained other design features representing the styles, aspirations, and social agendas of subsequent generations of park designers, users, and policy makers. Some of the design alterations to the park are recognized and embraced as part of the park's historical narrative. The Great Lawn is a prominent example of a significant modification to the "original" park. The replacement of a rectangular reservoir with an elliptical lawn and small pond in 1936 is generally accepted as integral to the present park plan and would most likely be defended by landscape historians and park athletes alike if it were threatened with removal.[2] The Great Lawn is one of several design features added to Central Park in the twentieth century that together constitute a venerable, but largely unheralded, tradition of modern and protomodern design in the historic park.

Modernism in park design is broadly defined for the purposes of this paper as a corollary of the architectural modernism most often associated with the International Style, which emerged and won gradual acceptance in this country in the 1930s. In American landscape design modernism first appears as editorial: with the critical writings and illustrations by landscape architect James Rose in *Pencil Points* magazine (later called *Progressive Architecture*), as well as commentary about European landscape modernism by author/practitioners like landscape architect Fletcher Steele in the 1930s and 1940s. It is generally accepted that the true flourishing of modernism in landscape architecture practice does not occur in this country until after World War II—considerably later than in architecture, notably with the works of landscape architects Thomas Church, Garrett Eckbo, and Dan Kiley. Central Park accords with this pattern, although it can be difficult to recognize modern contributions to the park because of the stylistically *retardataire* designs that were intended to be compatible with the historic park. Well in advance of preservation laws modern designers in Central Park attempted to honor the creators' vision. Then, as now, the precedent of Olmsted and Vaux was a paramount concern when additions and modifications to the park were contemplated. Recognition of modern design in Central Park is further complicated by distinct political influence on park design in New York City, an influence that delayed the emergence of effusive modernism until the 1960s, well after modernism had pervaded the corporate and residential landscape outside the park.

Central Park and the Playground Reform Movement

Playgrounds have been a part of the Central Park landscape beginning with the original Greensward Plan of 1858—albeit in somewhat different guises. The first Play Ground in Central Park was a small meadow located in the southwest corner of the park set aside by Olmsted and Vaux for organized children's activities. Outdoor exercise equipment was provided for children during favorable weather, and a small building dispensing such athletic equipment as balls and bats was erected at the periphery of the meadow. Other neighboring structures designed by Calvert Vaux, including the Dairy and the Kinderberg, were specifically intended as amenities for children. This part of the park, named the Children's Department, provided settings for children's education, health, relaxation, and amusement. This limited area remained the only designated place for children's play in Central Park until the 1920s despite lobbying efforts by progressive recreational reformers including individuals from the reform and settlement-house movements of New York City. Preservation-minded policy makers of Central Park, along with supporting civic organizations, were loathe to incorporate the structured playgrounds advocated by the reformers into the pastoral greensward of the park. The annual report of the New York City Department of Parks noted in 1914 that new playgrounds could not be carved out of existing parks because "the modern playground is a complete plant in itself and is most successful when segregated from a park."[3] Central Park trailed behind the rest of the city, and indeed most other cities in America, in providing structured spaces for children's play.

In the early decades of the twentieth century advocates for recreation reform were responsible for the construction of many parks designated for children's play throughout the city, but facing great opposition from park preservationists, they were successful in building only one equipped playground in Central Park. Philanthropist August Heckscher used his personal prestige to convince reluctant park officials to accept his gift of an equipped playground for Central Park in 1926.[4] Located within the original Play Ground in the southwest corner of the park, the Heckscher Playground, which featured slides, swings, jungle gyms, and a wading pool, remained the only equipped playground in Central Park until the mid-1930s. Urged on by the fiscal crisis of 1929 and an increase in public concern and political advocacy for the plight of indigent families, a new political administration—one with a more encompassing view of children's play—mandated equipped play areas in Central Park. Appointed by Mayor La Guardia in 1934, the reform administration of Parks Commissioner Robert Moses and his consultant landscape architect Gilmore D. Clarke began comprehensive planning for new playgrounds in Central Park. Some of the first of these new playgrounds were intended to serve children in parts of Central Park lacking any structured play amenities, particularly the northern reaches of the park. By 1941 the number of playgrounds in Central Park had been greatly expanded by the Moses administration to a total of twenty "marginal" playgrounds (so called because they were located along the edges of the park near the park wall) as well as some play areas located inside the park landscape.[5]

The Central Park playgrounds constructed by the administration of Moses featured sand boxes, playhouses, and standard steel play equipment including jungle gyms, swings, slides, and seesaws set in an asphalt landscape surrounded by benches and a picket fence. A limited amount of free space was allocated for running and tricycling. According to Commissioner Moses's own words, the primary purpose of the marginal playgrounds was to contain and restrict children rather than to enhance their play experiences: "These playgrounds are equipped with small-size swings, seesaws, slides and playhouses, shower basins, and benches. They are surfaced with a resilient asphalt preparation, which prevents digging and eliminates dust. They are fenced and the gates are locked at night. Located near the major entrances, they intercept children on the way into the park and provide a place in which excess energy can be worked off without damage to the park surroundings."[6] These designs from the 1930s remained virtually unmodified well into the 1960s— throughout the long tenure of Moses and his staff—despite the postwar publication

of new theories about children's play and psychological development. The groundbreaking texts by such child psychologists as R. D. Laing, Jean Piaget, Erik Erikson, and Bruno Bettelheim on child development were paralleled by new designs for children's play throughout war-ravaged Europe. These theories and designs were widely published in the United States and, although unheeded by the Moses parks administration, aroused the interest of artists, architects, and landscape architects as well as parents and advocates for children's play.

Adventure Playgrounds

During the era of postwar reconstruction "adventure playgrounds," also called "junk playgrounds" and "Robinson Crusoe playgrounds," became staples of progressive park planning across Europe. Using hammers, nails, saws, and mortar, albeit in a supervised, controlled setting, children at adventure playgrounds constructed their own play environment out of scrap wood, metal, and bricks. As early as 1931 Danish landscape architect C. Th. Sørensen advocated providing playgrounds with building and demolition materials after he observed children playing with refuse in junkyards and building sites. Refining his ideas, Sørensen noted that "when contemplating an adventure playground it is opportune to warn against too much supervision and too many arrangements for the children. It is my opinion that children ought to be free and by themselves to the greatest possible extent. . . . The object must be to give the children of the city a substitute for the rich possibilities for play which children in the country possess."[7]

Based on Sørensen's ideas, the first adventurelike playground, then known as a "skrammellegeplads," opened in 1943 at Emdrup, outside Copenhagen, during the German occupation of Denmark. Children were provided with a common area where modeling and constructional hobbies could be pursued, while adjacent open areas provided sites for children's building activities under the supervision of a playground leader. Once children had completed a building project they were encouraged to plant and tend small gardens around their creations until winter, when all the little houses would be dismantled. Visitors to the playground were astonished at the degree to which children had mastered technical building skills.[8]

After the war recurrent images of children playing in the wreckage of bombed buildings in Germany and Great Britain played a central role in the extension of the adventure-playground movement. The ideological symbolism of young people rebuilding Europe after the war undoubtedly helped to popularize what might otherwise have been viewed as an audacious experimental idea by which children were encouraged to play with potentially dangerous materials usually handled by adults. Publicity photographs of adventure playgrounds depicted scenes that would be unimaginable in playgrounds today: small children lighting massive bonfires, standing atop precarious towers of their own slap-dash construction, and cutting jagged-edged scraps of sheet metal. Despite the seeming invitation to injury defenders of the adventure-play concept noted that children tended to know their own limits, hence the surprisingly excellent safety records of adventure playgrounds. Defenders also pointed out that accidents tended to happen when, out of boredom, children attempted risky tricks on the fixed equipment of orthodox playgrounds.[9] Adventure playgrounds flourished in Europe after the war, particularly in Scandinavia, Switzerland, Great Britain, and Germany, and the concept soon spread to America.

Sculpture for Children's Play

Artists were interested in the possibilities inherent in the emerging field of designing for children—particularly in applying the developments in monumental abstract sculpture. The precedent for artists' involvement in designs for children's play was established by sculptor Isamu Noguchi's attempts to construct a sculptural children's play environment in New York City. Noguchi, one of America's most important artists, had been at the forefront of the environmental sculpture movement. He described how his experiments with playground design began as part of "a vision that the frontiers of sculpture might open up by relating it to the land and to real walkable space."[10] Noguchi's designs for playgrounds were unprecedented, a direct response to observations of how children playfully interact with landscape. He was also among the first to recognize the need for playgrounds that would foster a continuum of play experience in an environment of total design—an approach in marked contrast with the convention of aimlessly sited, isolated pieces of equipment, each geared to a single imagination-restricting function. (Antonio Gaudi, the visionary Catalan architect, had earlier explored somewhat similar ideas.)[11] Noguchi's earliest foray into playground design was the *Play Mountain* of 1933, intended for an entire city block in New York City, a transformation of one of his monumental sculptures into an environment for play with steps of all sizes, a slide with water in summer, and a larger one for sledding in winter. Noguchi noted that "*Play Mountain* was the kernel out of which have grown all my ideas relating sculpture to the earth. It is also the progenitor of playgrounds as sculptural landscapes."[12] A model of the play sculpture was shown to Parks Commissioner Moses and, Noguchi noted, "gained his perpetual antagonism."[13]

Moses frequently cited safety issues as a reason for rejecting new ideas for children's play, motivating Noguchi in 1941 to create a proposal for a Contoured Playground that he believed contained no elements that might cause injury to anyone. Although the Moses administration feigned interest in testing the playground in Central Park, it, too, was never built, ostensibly because of budget cuts due to America's impending involvement in World War II.[14] In 1951, when construction of the United Nations complex resulted in the relocation of a playground, neighbors commissioned Noguchi, in collaboration with architect Julian Whittlesey, to design the new one. The playground proposal was touted by architecture journals; Moses, however, rejected the innovative design with a quip—"We know what works"—and built instead a standard playground designed by Gilmore D. Clarke.[15] The Museum of Modern Art in New York City subsequently exhibited Noguchi's playground models, commending the scheme as "a particularly striking illustration of the possibilities of stimulating the child's sense of space and form through a playground designed as architectural sculpture."[16]

Although Noguchi's proposals for sculpted play environments had been repeatedly rebuffed by Moses, the drawings and models for these pioneering designs exerted great influence through exhibitions and publications. Directly influenced by the fracas in the design community surrounding the rejected proposal for the United Nations playground, The Museum of Modern Art initiated a design competition for children's play equipment in 1954. The Play Sculptures competition and an exhibition of winning entries were sponsored by *Parents* magazine and Creative Playthings, Inc., a manufacturer of inventive designs for children's play, with the idea that some of the entries would result in buildable prototypes. The exhibition brought the reexamination of children's play experiences to the forefront of the art and design world, legitimizing the artistic endeavor of designing children's playgrounds. Entries to the museum competition shared many themes that showed the influence and adaptation of European theories on children's play. These included continuous play, cooperative/interactive play, and imaginative play. The European adventure playground, in which children created their own environments with hammers, nails, and wood, was reinterpreted by the American designers as sculpted, abstract modular units that children could arrange to suit their whims. The most important concept in the competition exhibit was the integration of play and the environment. Although the experiment was originally envisioned as resulting in marketable play equipment, designers overwhelmingly attempted to blur the spatial distinction between object and landscape and instead created play "environments" in which several play features were integrated within one design. Undoubtedly influenced by Noguchi's seminal design work—combined with the programmatic concerns of children's play advocates—these designs heralded the possibility, as yet unrealized in New York City parks, of reinventing children's playgrounds.

Although the organizers of The Museum of Modern Art exhibition had intended that some of the designs eventually find their way into park playgrounds, Moses was steadfast in his resistance to change. Aside from the occasional introduction of novelty play equipment, like the metal stagecoaches and rocketships that were produced in the 1950s, Central Park playgrounds remained virtually unchanged from the 1930s.[17] The construction of the fanciful Hans Christian Andersen (1957) and Alice in Wonderland (1959) statues in Central Park persuaded some critics that the Parks Department would perhaps become more receptive to the idea of sculpted play environments for children. But in 1959, in a letter to Creative Playthings, Inc., the New York City Parks Department reiterated the Commissioner's restrictive directives regarding sculpture for children: "We have always permitted children to play on park sculpture which represents persons, animals or fictitious characters well known to most children. However, our decision to permit children to play on this sculpture does not mean that we endorse play sculptures for general use in the park-system playgrounds. There is an essential difference between Hans Christian Andersen, Alice in Wonderland, and your stone, fiberglass, and steel Play Sculptured equipment. We have discussed this matter with you before and see no reason for changing the type of equipment we use in the playgrounds in the New York City Park System."[18] Frank Caplan, president of Creative Playthings, Inc., felt that Moses was ideologically opposed to modern design: "He just doesn't like that 'modern stuff.' Give him a piece of realism and he sees art in it." This despite the fact that children prefer abstract sculpture, a fact "verified by every Park Commissioner in the Country."[19]

Even though Central Park's Hans Christian Andersen and Alice in Wonderland statues proved to be immensely popular attractions for children, the representational sculptures were continually criticized by advocates of modern design. *Art in America* magazine, in a 1967 cover story devoted to recent designs for children's play, noted that "although sculptors are increasingly being encouraged to experiment with playground design, the mere participation of a noted sculptor is no guarantee of good results. José de Creeft's Alice in Wonderland group in Central Park, for example, is from every standpoint one of the most atrociously miscon-

A model shows the final proposal for Levy Memorial Playground, Riverside Park at 103rd Street, New York City, Isamu Noguchi and Louis I. Kahn, 1965.

PHOTO BY SOICHI SUNAMI, THE MUSEUM OF MODERN ART, NEW YORK

ceived devices in existence. . . . The whole lamentable enterprise is at once too literal to stimulate the imagination and too 'unreadable' for a literal piece."[20] The magazine bemoaned the fixed interpretation of representational sculpture, which precluded imaginative play: These types of statues "have little appeal for the kid who wants to play astronaut, race driver, or fireman."[21] Lost in the criticism was the boldly modern landscape setting designed by landscape architect Hideo Sasaki. It featured a spiraling paved platform inscribed with quotations from Lewis Carroll and custom-designed geometric benches. Even the plantings were treated as architectonic elements that were heavily pruned and shaped to reinforce the circuitous, self-contained fantasy world of Alice, a world entirely removed from the naturalistic landscape palette of Central Park. Because of the popularity of the sculpture the landscape setting has been meticulously maintained and today presents one of the best preserved examples of modern public landscape design from the postwar era in New York City.

The Playground Revolution

When Lady Allen of Hurtwood, the renowned British landscape architect, playground designer, and children's play advocate, conducted a tour of New York City playgrounds in the early 1960s, she was so distressed by what she saw that she urged parents to "put in a claim against the city fathers for emotional damage to their children because they failed to provide suitable and exciting playgrounds for them."[22] New York City Parks had remained woefully behind the times regarding innovations in children's playgrounds. However, in the early 1960s several philanthropic foundations and advocacy groups began to lay the foundation for the introduction of imaginative designs for New York City playgrounds at venues other than city parks. Notable among these groups were the Junior Council of The Museum of Modern Art, the J. M. Kaplan Fund, the Vincent Astor Foundation, the Avalon Foundation, and the New York Community Trust. Advocacy groups included the Citizens Committee for Children, the Council for Parks and Playgrounds, and the Park Association of New York City.[23] These organizations enlisted the support of corporations and city politicians and fostered new ideas for play by sponsoring exhibitions, publications, and even the construction of some model playgrounds.

In 1964 the Park Association of New York City sponsored an international student design competition and subsequent exhibition entitled New Ideas for City Parks. Whitney North Seymour, Jr., president of the Park Association, noted in the exhibition booklet that "the playgrounds of New York City are unfortunately characterized by sterility. They have achieved a set of engineering standards—reasonably indestructible and requiring low maintenance—but they have done little to raise young hearts and minds to excitement, fantasy, and sheer joy."[24] On opening night the enthusiasm engendered by the exhibition's student entries was dampened by the presence of New York City Parks Commissioner Newbold Morris, who carried on the policies of the Moses administration in his absence. (Moses had resigned in 1960 to plan the New York World's Fair of 1964.) Morris winced as he viewed the exhibition, noting unforeseen dangers in the experimental designs: "Most of these creative people never think of these things—and I never did either until I became Commissioner of Parks."[25] Confirming the negative attributes about playgrounds cited by the Park Association, Morris emphasized that existing rugged play equipment and play surfaces were tried and true solutions for the vandalism and maintenance concerns that, he believed, plagued park playgrounds. Nevertheless, the Park Association was undeterred in its ultimate goal to actually build playgrounds based on innovative ideas: "Above all, the basic fact is that many new ideas for city playgrounds exist. The challenge is to get them into practical application now for use and enjoyment by today's city children."[26] The Park Association proved particularly resourceful in finding spaces to showcase new designs, sponsoring the construction of model play environments on several vacant lots in Harlem and in Brooklyn. The designs were contributed by a variety of individuals, firms, and institutions, including architect I.M. Pei; landscape architects Robert Nichols, Zion & Breen, and M. Paul Friedberg & Associates; and the Columbia University School of Architecture. The designs, known as vest-pocket parks, attempted to go beyond the routine of scattered play equipment and instead create spaces that could serve a variety of programmatic needs like art-making, performance, picnics, relaxation, group games, and imaginative play.[27] Some designs showed the influence of the adventure playgrounds of Europe by providing places where children could create their own play environments with found materials.

Although the New York City Parks Department was resistant to change, other city agencies began to respond to the call for new ideas. The New York City Housing Authority, Board of Education, and Planning Commission were willing to experiment with modern concepts for children's outdoor play, commissioning, in collaboration with philanthropic foundations and advocacy groups, new designs to enrich the ground plane at selected housing developments, city schools, and city lots. The Housing Authority already had a long tradition in New York of sponsoring modern design, influenced by European planning precedents. In 1961 the Housing Authority began a program of redesigning outdoor spaces at existing housing projects. Architect Albert Mayer of the firm Mayer, Whittlesey & Glass was hired to design new plazas for Jefferson Houses and Franklin Houses, both located in East Harlem. Mayer— an unsung hero of enlightened open-space planning in New York City—created play centers for the public-housing developments incorporating sand, water, climbing equipment, benches, and shade structures as integrated abstracted compositions. Children exulted in the variety of play, parents and other residents appreciated the shady refuge, and critics praised the artfulness of the endeavor.[28] Mayer's designs were undoubtedly influenced by his partner Julian Whittlesey, who had earlier collaborated with Noguchi on playground proposals, including the famous unbuilt design for a playground at the United Nations (from 1951).

In 1963 the Vincent Astor Foundation commissioned landscape architect M. Paul Friedberg to redesign the open spaces at the Carver Houses, an existing New York City Housing Authority property in East Harlem. *Progressive Architecture* noted that "a desolate landscape of concrete, asphalt, and chained-off 'grass' spaces has been replaced by a usable, multifaceted public court that the inhabitants have taken to their hearts."[29] The existing plaza was regraded to create a varied terrain where such constructed elements as amphitheater seating were integrated with the landscape. The play spaces and sitting areas of Mayer's earlier work in East Harlem were reinterpreted by Friedberg, who said that he sought to avoid the "insubstantial" look of Mayer's plazas by using more durable construction materials.[30] Friedberg's most important and influential design for the Housing Authority was the Jacob Riis Houses Plaza (opened in 1966), also financed by the Vincent Astor Foundation. Here, programmatic requirements of seating areas, climbing equipment, water features, and performance spaces were completely integrated with the hardscape of the plaza through a variety of forms and level changes. The play areas incorporated wood, cobblestone, and metal into sculpted landforms reminiscent of Noguchi's pioneering work. Riis Plaza was considered a triumph of urban landscape design and, along with his topographically sculpted playground for the Board of Education at Public School 166 in Manhattan (opened in 1967), established Friedberg as the one of the foremost designers of recreational spaces in the United States.[31]

One of the most famous and influential designs for a park playground from this era was the unbuilt Levy Memorial Playground designed collaboratively by Noguchi and architect Louis Kahn. Intended for a hilly site in Riverside Park, the design incorporated the existing topography into the proposal for slides and climbing equipment seemingly sculpted out of the earth. The sculpted play equipment was reminiscent of natural landforms like volcanoes as well as of architectonic creations like pyramids. The forms were intended to be nonspecific but suggestive—to inspire children's imaginative play in conjunction with physical exercise. Although the design was ultimately rejected by the city, in this case largely because of neighborhood opposition, the plans and model for the playground were published and exhibited and, like Noguchi's previous playground designs, unquestionably suggested a prototype for subsequent playground designers. Noguchi announced that he was exhausted by his protracted struggle to build a playground in New York City and that he would not attempt to do so again. The successful reception of innovative designs for playgrounds in city parks would have to wait for a complete change of the city's political administration.

A New Administration / A New Attitude Toward Play

When John Lindsay succeeded in his bid for mayor of New York City in November 1965 a progressive attitude toward parks was assured with the appointment of Thomas Hoving as Parks Commissioner. Young, flamboyant, and enthusiastic, Hoving was willing to experiment with new ideas for city parks and playgrounds: "We want ideas that will be so revolutionary as to create a vicious controversy. When people begin attacking us for being *too* far out, that's when we'll know we are really trying out constructive new plans that our children deserve."[32]

Hoving was committed to revitalizing city parks, and his administration immediately began a campaign to democratize parks for a wider audience and to reinterpret the role of parks in the modern city. The Moses parks administration had transformed the concept of the pastoral park into the recreational park; now the park would be redefined as a theater in which people were both spectators and participants. Eager to welcome a new generation to city parks, Hoving's administration envisioned Central Park as a site for events called "happenings." Happenings were intended to involve a wide range of people in the concept of a public park and to foster public stewardship of parks. Sanctioned happenings included kite-flying spectacles, outdoor art festivals, costumed pageants, concerts, and dancing as well as events intended to acquaint people with the natural and human histories of the park including celebrations of the seasons. Essentially publicity events that generated notice for the parks department, happenings dramatically underscored the administration's new attitude toward the concept of a city park.

Looking back on his career, Hoving noted that "the most significant thing we accomplished is the entire change of direction in design."[33] Designers who participated in Hoving's transformation of parks were encouraged to be experimental in providing new amenities and updating old ones. Ada Louise Huxtable, architecture critic for *The New York Times,* noted that Hoving's administration signaled "an all-out attack on a kind of repetitive, conservative design associated with the Parks Department since the Depression days of the WPA that critics have alternately called naive or Neanderthal."[34] Hoving also denounced park construction from the previous thirty years as "hideous" and "disgraceful" and declared that the time had come to bring to city parks "the excitement and creativity of modern design. . . . Now we can seek out the finest architects in our country and abroad to bring imagination and vision to the city's planning."[35] To accomplish his parks revolution Hoving courted an international roster of famous contemporary architects and landscape architects that included Philip Johnson, Lawrence Halprin, Marcel Breuer, Edward Larrabee Barnes, Kenzo Tange, and Felix Candela.

Hoving's emphasis on new design was not a repudiation of historic park design, but rather a reinterpretation of how to approach historic designed landscapes. His administration brought a fresh perspective to issues of landscape history, preservation, and design integrity that inaugurated the officially sanctioned historic preservation of designed landscapes in New York City. Hoving believed that by reinventing city parks his administration was continuing the innovative traditions of the Olmsted and Vaux era as well as concurrently creating a forum to prevent any permanent alterations to their historic designs. Hoving had previously been curator of the Cloisters Museum in New York City and would later become famous as curator of the Metropolitan Museum of Art, and because of this background in art and architectural history he treated historic city parks as works of art; indeed, he even created the position of Curator of Central Park, to which he appointed the eminent architectural historian Henry Hope Reed. Hoving criticized recent park design compared with that of Olmsted and Vaux: "We've got to get back to the concept that a park is a work of art. Every portion, every piece contributes to a harmony. Everything should be detailed—the banisters, railings, contourings, the curvatures of the chairs. In the old days they thought of texture, they considered the landscape as a painter [would]. Today, that's all but disappeared."[36]

Hoving's promotion of the artistry of park design through his administration's flamboyant happenings, his patronage of famous contemporary designers, and his appointment of a park historian validated the historic integrity of designed landscapes as worthy of the same respect and preservation accorded to historic works of architecture. Commissioning new designs to be incorporated into historic parks, Hoving declared that his administration would "bring back the opportunity for imagination, taste, and creative design that existed in the nineteenth century"[37] Hoving's concept, consistent with modernist architectural doctrine, was that the best way to add to a historic design was to seek completely new designs that were of equally high artistic quality yet stylistically resonant with one's own time. The Moses administration had promoted historic contextualism in Central Park by commissioning new designs that attempted to incorporate aspects of the park's historic details, usually through mimetic iconography of what were considered to be the park's original "Victorian" structures. Even modernist designs for city parks from the 1950s and 1960s tended to display the hallmarks of a distilled historicism, largely under the influence of Gilmore D. Clarke and other designers who had trained in the Beaux Arts tradition. With Hoving's administration new designs for historic city parks abandoned traditional park decorum and instead promoted geometric abstraction, experimental technology, and expressive use of materials. Contextualism was now thought to be accomplished by responding directly to the park landscape, rather than mimicking park structures, as Hoving attempted to bring the precepts of environmental design to New York City parks.

Hoving was particularly determined to reinvent park playgrounds and fervently criticized the Parks Department's legacy of poorly planned children's play areas: "Each park, each playground has got to be unique. Look at the playgrounds now—they have the same asphalt, the same fences, the same play areas and comfort stations. Look at that hideous concrete and asphalt WPA-Mussolini style! . . . [Moses] built 700 playgrounds. Great! But the man has no interest in environmental design."[38] Under Hoving's administration sophisticated ideas for children's play—previously rejected for city parks and instead relegated to privately financed venues at vest-pocket parks, Housing Authority sites, and Board of Education schoolyards—now became models for municipal park planning. Hoving had earlier outlined his strategy for bringing innovative playgrounds to city parks in a policy paper that he wrote for Lindsay's campaign. In addition to advocating more vest-pocket parks and continued improvements to Housing Authority projects Lindsay called for the introduction of adventure playgrounds in New York City, noting that "these playgrounds have recently captured the imagination of some forward-looking individuals in this country."[39] The policy paper described the new playgrounds as a dramatic contrast "to the traditional asphalt surfacing and immovable slides, swings, seesaws, and jungle gyms of playgrounds as we know them all over the city" and praised the cooperative play fostered by adventure playgrounds, play that "has been shown to develop in the children an intensified sense of community—of working together, working for others, and building for those less able (the younger ones). This activity inspires independence, courage, and initiative."[40] Advocates for children's play finally had a political administration that was receptive to their ideas, and it was in this progressive milieu that the adventure-playground concept was brought to Central Park.

The Adventure Playground

The Adventure Playground of Central Park, which opened in May 1967, marked the Hoving administration's bold attempt to accommodate progressive theories of children's play that had already influenced play areas at facilities outside city parks. The site for the new playground was one of the original Moses-era marginal playgrounds located along Central Park West, just north of the Tavern on the Green restaurant at the West 67th Street entrance to the park. This playground and the adjacent landscape were practically hallowed ground on the Upper West Side of Manhattan as the site of what had become known as the Battle of Central Park in 1956. As the staging ground for the "battle" the playground had acquired a certain significance.

The battle began in 1956 when a contractor accidentally left his construction drawings in Central Park while he went to fetch some lunch.[41] A local resident was taking a walk in Central Park in the vicinity of the Tavern on the Green and spotted the construction drawings lying on a rock. She was horrified to see that a massive expansion was planned for the restaurant parking lot, obliterating trees and parkland adjacent to her neighborhood playground. Several of her neighbors worked in media, and news of the planned demolition was soon known citywide. Questions were raised about whether the City should be subsidizing a parking lot in a public park for a private restaurateur, who happened to be an acquaintance of the Parks Commissioner. Moses's tactical response was to commandeer bulldozers in the middle of the night and begin uprooting the trees. Neighbors along Central Park West were awakened by the noise and responded with a human line of defense. Sleepy children positioned alongside their mothers to block the path of bulldozers in Central Park provided dramatic subject material for photographs in the New York daily newspapers the following day.

The standoff between parents and the New York City Parks Department ended as Moses was forced to confront heightened media allegations of corruption concerning the contract for the Tavern on the Green restaurant. Moses abandoned his plans for a parking lot and offered to build an additional playground at the demolition site as a conciliatory gesture to the parents. The Battle of Central Park marked the beginning of the end of Moses's political career. Moses, who had initially built his career providing state-of-the-art recreational facilities throughout New York City to serve an expanding metropolitan population, was now portrayed by the media as a destroyer of parks and neighborhoods. The victorious parents, who had become acquainted with one another through the battle, continued to meet regularly at the neighborhood playground. Six years later, when a child was seriously hurt in the playground after a fall from a slide, some of the parents decided that something should be done to prevent further accidents. The playground featured isolated steel play equipment in an asphalt lot surrounded by a picket fence, a playground typical of the Moses era. What had once been standard now appeared inadequate to savvy neighborhood parents, who knew of innovative developments in children's play areas outside of city parks. Galvanized into activism by the legacy of the successful battle, the parents formed an organization, the Mothers' Committee to Improve the West 67th Street Playground (the name would later be changed to the Committee for a Creative Playground), and petitioned the city for an improved, safer playground.

The parents found that the recently appointed commissioner, Hoving, would lend his support and advice, although sufficient city funds were not available to renovate the playground. Instead, he sought sponsorship from private philanthropic organizations that had previously funded progressive playgrounds at Department of City Planning, Housing Authority, and Board of Education sites. Meanwhile, the Estée and Joseph Lauder Foundation, funded by the Estée Lauder cosmetics company, approached the city about the possibility of creating a prototype adventure playground in a city park. The Lauder family had been inspired by Lady Allen of Hurtwood when she visited the United States in 1965. Leonard Lauder, president of the company, and his wife Evelyn had young children and were well aware of how inadequate park playgrounds contributed to the diminution of city living and to the lure of suburbs for young families: "We first wanted to do this several years ago when many of our friends were fleeing the city because they thought New York wasn't the place to bring up children. We decided to build several of these to give the city just this little lift."[42] The Parks Department accepted the Lauders' gift and determined that the Central Park playground at West 67th Street would provide a prominent location for an innovative experimental design. The Mothers' Committee was considered to be an ideal constituent group, given their initiative and resolve to renovate the playground and the potential to involve the entire community in the process. *Art in America* magazine commented on the phenomenon in 1967: "Hoving's impact on the nation's playground design cannot be evaluated with any accuracy, but obviously it has been enormous. Within months of his appointment men and women—even the children themselves—were imbued with a sense of participation that had never been possible under the previous administration."[43]

The Lauder Foundation commissioned the young architect Richard Dattner to design the new playground in consultation with the coalition of parents. Dattner, a native of Buffalo, New York, had studied at the Architectural Association in London and at the Massachusetts Institute of Technology, from which he received his Bachelor of Architecture degree in 1960. The following year he was awarded a traveling fellowship for study in Greece and Sicily by the American Institute of Architects. At the time of the playground commission Dattner was just twenty-seven years old and had only recently designed a new cosmetics lab and plant for the Estée Lauder Company in Melville, New York (designed in conjunction with the firm Davis, Brody & Associates).[44] Landforms, which would prove integral to the design of the Adventure Playground, were strategically employed by the designers of the Lauder factory to dramatically and functionally resolve the difficult siting alongside the Long Island Expressway. To passing motorists the sleek white porcelain-enameled facade of the structure appeared to float above a sodded berm that served as a conceptual and actual rampart, visually protecting the complex and also dampening noise from the highway.

Designing the Adventure Playground: Concept and Process

To prepare for designing the Adventure Playground Dattner consulted recent advances in the study of children's play, assisted by his wife, who was studying to become a clinical psychologist. The understanding of children's play had advanced from the notion of children's letting off steam to the realization that play is one of the chief ways that children learn about their world. "Playgrounds aren't for play, they're for learning," noted Dattner. "In a broad and democratic sense, learning is predicated on play, and play in turn is one way children develop intelligence."[45] Dattner's understanding of progressive theories about children's play was directly applied to the design program. He identified seven play precepts for the playground derived from Jean Piaget's studies of stages in children's intellectual development and from R.D. Laing's writings on the creative interaction of the individual and the environment: Experience, Control of Experience, Graduated Challenge, Choice, Exercise of Fantasy, Separation from Adults, and Expressive Play. Dattner strove to get inside the seemingly impenetrable minds of his young clients, the children who would play in the new playground; to understand how children re-create their environment through play; and to incorporate this into the playground design: "The place where children play is a sort of magic circle, outside and separate from the rest of the world; it has its own time, which cannot be measured by our clocks. Within this all is transformed and controlled by imagination, and a perfect world is possible."[46]

Dattner embarked on an anthropological investigation of children playing in New York City, paying special attention to how children interacted with found objects and urban fixtures. He was attuned to the ways that children carved out recreation space in a somewhat forbidding urban environment as he photographed children on city streets building with discarded tin cans, swinging from fire-escape ladders, and jumping on abandoned sofas in empty lots. He noted how children's propensity for imaginative play operated in the urban environment: how a curbside gutter after a rainfall can become a stream to a child and how a refuse pile can become a mountain. He also observed children's tendency to incorporate disparate urban fixtures into an arena of contiguous play, transforming neighboring railings, steps, ledges, and fire hydrants into a miniature landscape for climbing, exploring, balancing, sliding, and sitting. These observations fueled Dattner's design for a playground that would function as a small-scale landscape, which children's imaginations could transform into a variety of stages for group or solo play. Play equipment would be integrated with the playground landscape to create what Dattner called "a landscape for kids," an environment for imaginative play that simultaneously could accommodate children's need for physical activity.[47] Acknowledging his debt to Noguchi, Dattner envisioned a playground of contiguous sculpted landforms that would present graduated physical challenges for children, including climbing, sliding, jumping, stretching and balancing, as well as provide shelter and enclosure for less rambunctious play.

Parents had their own ideas about what the new playground should include, as noted by *The New York Times* in 1966: "Mothers are rising up to demand consultative rights on the design of playgrounds in which they and their children will be penned for significant parts of their lives."[48] Dattner worked directly with neighborhood parents on the design for the new playground, mindful of the recent debacle that had halted the Noguchi/Kahn playground design: "Although never built, this playground had a considerable influence on subsequent playgrounds, including the Adventure Playground. In addition to its outstanding design, the doomed project yielded one very important lesson: The community must be fully involved in a project from its inception."[49] Dattner worked in sketches and models at a series of meetings with parents to determine how concerns and suggestions could be incorporated into the design at an early stage. The director of design from Hoving's parks administration, Arthur Rosenblatt, observed: "This sort of interchange is fostered by the Parks Department's Community Relations Division, established out of the belief that only by discovering what the people want can the designers develop programs for new buildings or parks which are uniquely suited to their location."[50]

Safe play was a paramount concern for most parents, as typical park playgrounds were considered to be invitations to accidents. The chief safety flaw of playgrounds from the Moses era was the possibility of a free fall from equipment onto a hard surface. For example, the slides and seesaws were freestanding, which meant that children could accidentally tumble over the sides and fall through the air before hitting the asphalt. Dattner, like Friedberg and Noguchi before him, proposed sculpted play equipment that had no possibility of free fall because slides and ladders would be incorporated directly into the structure. The use of sand, usually confined to a sand-box, would be expanded to provide a broad area of soft surface to cushion falls around the climbing equipment. However, rather than try to entirely eradicate any possibility for accidents at the playground, Dattner impressed upon the parents the need for certain degrees of challenge to be built into the play equipment. Dattner believed that children know their own limits and that by incorporating equipment that presented graduated challenges children of different ages and abilities would be safely accommodated. Toddlers, who do not know their own limits, would be deterred from the climbing equipment by an initial step that would be out of their reach. Dattner noted that parents "were particularly helpful in discussing the right heights for steps and where I should have railings."[51] Dattner's perceptive design proposal verified his understanding of child psychology: "A playground therefore should present a series of challenges, ranging from simple things that toddlers can master to ones that challenge older and more experienced children. There should be continuity, so that each child always has the dual experience of having mastered some aspects of his environment while knowing there are other aspects that he may still aspire to master. As in adult life, the individual who feels he has accomplished everything and the one who is so overwhelmed that he is unable to accomplish anything have both reached a point where further growth and development are impossible."[52]

The adventure play concept was also introduced at the community meetings to parents who enthusiastically embraced the idea as a departure from the usual

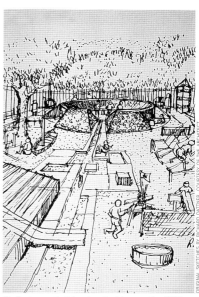

Preliminary sketch, view looking south, 1966   *Preliminary sketch, view looking north, 1966*

ORIGINAL SKETCHES BY RICHARD DATTNER, COURTESY OF THE ARCHITECT

city playgrounds. Following the lead of European adventure playgrounds, parents sought a play supervisor who could provide assistance when the children requested it but also allow them the option of playing by themselves. Dattner noted that "a supervisor should possess the good qualities of a parent without the parent's emotional stake in the children's performance."[53] At the Adventure Playground the play supervisor would also be responsible for directing children's art instruction, story hours, and theatrical events.[54] Understanding that this type of playground would require enhanced maintenance and supervision, the Lauders' foundation agreed to endow a maintenance fund in addition to paying for construction, for a total cost of $85,000, provided that the community raise $12,000 to hire the play supervisor. Dattner later observed that the decision to make the community financially responsible for the play supervisor was a wise one because it fostered neighborhood stewardship for the playground: "It continually reminded the community that their efforts had secured the project in the first place and were needed to ensure its success."[55]

Dattner understood that a full-fledged adventure playground in which small children handled tools and rough-edged objects was unlikely to be realized in a New York City park and that to an American audience the European-style playgrounds resembled junkyards. Leonard Lauder, as benefactor of the playground, elaborated on this view: "What is appropriate for a bombed-out site in the heart of London is not appropriate for probably the greatest masterpiece of landscape architecture, which is Central Park, and I would no more think of putting in bricks and tires and loose pieces of wood in Central Park than I would of putting in an elaborate structure in the middle of a bombed-out area."[56] However, by observing children playing in the urban environment and considering alternative outlets for this play Dattner was able to translate European adventure-play principles into a fresh context that would also be acceptable to his sponsor, as well as to parents and politicians. He had noted how children liked to build, mold, and dig and then considered how he could accommodate this in a relatively safe and renewable format. Similar to his ideas for integrating disparate pieces of play equipment into a continuous landscape of play he proposed expanding the standard playground sandbox into the medium of play for the entire playground. The large expanse of sand would create a renewable adventure-type material for children's building activities, in addition to providing an ideal surface to safely accommodate jumping and falling from play equipment.

PHOTOGRAPH OF MODEL COURTESY OF THE ARCHITECT

Final model for the Adventure Playground by Richard Dattner, 1966

Water also became an important play element in Dattner's design: "The most interesting place in a typical playground is the drinking fountain, the site of an endless stream of activity—and water. Swings and slides may lie idle after a while, but there are unlimited possibilities for play with water."[57] The standard splashing pool from the Moses-era playground was retained in Dattner's design and surrounded by amphitheater seating, integrating it into the surrounding play environment and providing a place for parents to sit close by their children at play. The runoff water from the pool would be collected into a sculpted water channel extending through the middle of the playground. Dattner later modified the design to incorporate a series of shallow pools and spillways where children could temporarily dam the water flow and observe simple hydraulic principles. Because sand would inevitably be dumped into the water by children, the sequence of pools was also intended to trap the sand before it could clog the drain. Precedents for the water channel are as old as the gardens of the Alhambra and as recent as work by Halprin and Kahn. Kahn's water channel for the Salk Institute in La Jolla, California, completed in 1965, quite likely provided a model for Dattner's employment of the water passage as the architectonic spine of the composition at the Adventure Playground. Dattner was able to translate precedents of water as expressive and transcendental elements in landscape design into an adventure-play medium that would be controlled by the children: "If you had nothing else, just dirt and water, or sand and water, they would be the two ideal play materials. A big sand pit with a big water pool next to it would probably meet ninety percent of the kids' needs."[58] The Adventure Playground would provide city children with an urban stream in which to splash, spray, sail paper boats, and gather buckets of water to wet the sand for building activities.

In a more direct nod to European adventure-play concepts Dattner also designed a series of modular wooden building panels, which were notched to interlock with each other. The panels were conceptually similar to those proposed in The Museum of Modern Art's 1954 playground exhibition and were perhaps directly influenced by construction toys from European "play parks."[59] Related to adventure playgrounds, play parks offered a sanitized version of adventure play with modular constructional materials that could be assembled by children without hammers, nails, and saws. While children's constructions at adventure playgrounds would remain throughout an entire season, the structures built by children at play parks could be taken apart at the end of each day. Dattner's play panels likewise enabled children to create small-scale stable shelters, which could later be dismantled and reassembled

into new configurations. The panels had rounded edges for safety and were painted with boldly colored patterns of targets and chevrons, resonant of "supergraphics" design from that era. Dattner also provided smaller wooden building blocks in compatible bold color schemes to inspire building activity by younger children who would not be able to wield the panels. The play supervisor, in addition to overseeing children's play, would be responsible for distributing and encouraging the use of the mobile construction materials. When not in use, the blocks and panels, along with books and sand-building toys, could be stored inside one of the climbing structures.

In addition to innovative European playgrounds Dattner was able to draw upon the considerable history of progressive playground design from New York City. The Noguchi/Kahn design for a playground in Riverside Park had only recently been presented and played a pivotal role in the spatial conception of Dattner's design for the Adventure Playground. Friedberg's programmatic conception of continuous play, demonstrated by his recently opened Jacob Riis Houses playground, also influenced the relationship between the play elements in Dattner's design. However, while Friedberg's work attempted to express natural form in manmade materials, Dattner was more interested in creating architectonic compositions of nature abstracted into pure geometry. Dattner's background as an architect determined his ordered, architectonic approach to the playground, compared with the expressionistic playgrounds of landscape architect Friedberg or the organic forms of sculptor Noguchi.

The philosophy of architect Louis Kahn was perhaps the most important influence on Dattner's design. Like Kahn, Dattner had traveled to Europe and visited ancient archaeological sites at which he observed classical architecture bereft of polychromy and stripped to essential geometric components. The compositions created by the juxtapositions of simple geometric shapes informed Kahn's notion of space and program in design. Kahn advocated the use of rational, primal geometry combined in unconventional arrangements to allow for spontaneity—or what Kahn believed to be the self-determination of choice in the built landscape. Kahn proposed a complex arrangement of forms that were joined to create "availabilities" or unprogrammed space: "The architect's job, in my opinion, is to find those spaces where the availabilities, not yet here, and those that are already here, can have better environments for their maturing into."[60] Dattner was able to apply Kahn's teachings to his understanding of childhood development to create a playground that was architecturally and programmatically designed to accommodate children's ability to continuously transform their environment through imaginative play: "The next best thing to a playground that children design themselves is one devised for them that opens option and opportunity to create their own play places."[61]

Dattner designed the Adventure Playground using a clay model, a mutable medium for interaction with his clients, the neighborhood parents. The clay also suggested how the children, the ultimate clients, would later be inspired to mold their own environments. The playground maquette provided a small-scale model for the finished playground, which itself would provide a large-scale model for children's building activities and imaginations. Dattner's final model resembled an archaeological ruin of an ancient city, scaled to a child's size. The sculpted "equipment" of the playground suggested miniaturized mountains, volcanoes, forts, spaceships, and pyramids that appeared to be rising out of the sand, encouraging children to sculpt and mold the sand into an even more miniature environment. The playground model showed how the landforms, to be constructed of concrete and granite blocks, would be integrated into the ground plane of the playground, while the wooden climbing features—including a large pyramid, geodesic climbing poles, and a treehouse—would read as structures perched on top of the landscape. The wooden climbing elements were composed with angled geometry like triangles and octagons in contrast to the rounded forms of the masonry features. All of the masonry landforms designed by Dattner were simple circuitous shapes, easily replicated in sand and, indeed, apparently inspired by the slope-sided walls of sand-castle construction: the effect of gravity on unstable matter.

Construction and Opening

Dattner's model and sketches appeared in *The New York Times* and other news-papers that covered the progress of the design process as a newsworthy event. Construction began in the fall of 1966 with the demolition of the old playground. At a press conference Commissioner Hoving exultantly announced that the new playground would do away with all the "Mickey Mouse rinky-dink junk we've had all these years."[62] Dattner also had little regard for the old play equipment: "The only standard equipment I've found useful is slides, which I use with the landscape of other forms. I think that the concrete animals and pipe rocketships are useless and dangerous, as are most metal swings and seesaws."[63] The only elements from the old playground retained in Dattner's design were the perimeter fencing and benches, as well as a small, rather charming tool shed, part of Moses's original "Victorianesque" vocabulary of park furnishings. Granite block from the old playground was also excavated at the demolition site and reused to create climbing surfaces on the new sculpted-masonry play equipment. The playground's vocabulary of concrete, granite block, and raw timbers adopted the aesthetics of New Brutalism as applied to land-scape architecture, a style that was the polar opposite of Moses's historically derived designs. The wood-grained pattern imprinted on the concrete walls, a hallmark of Brutalist design detail, was actually contributed by workmen from the Kreisler-Borg Construction Company. Although Dattner specified different sized strips of lumber to create a pattern that embraced chance, the workmen's innate sense of order precluded a random arrangement, and they developed an elaborate system for creating symmetrical patterns. Dattner realized that this misunderstanding was itself part of the design process and an example of exerting choice, an activity that the playground was designed to accommodate.

The completed playground, which opened to the public in the spring of 1967, presented a group of varied and related geometrically sculpted landforms surrounding a large central space. The enclosing elements and spaces created between the elements were designed so that children could feel that they were entering their own private world. The term "adventure" also took on a more literal meaning at the playground as children discovered tunnels and ladders with which they could explore the insides of some of the landforms. A child could choose among myriad activities and places within the playground while still being part of a larger group. Dattner noted that "the whole playground is designed to give the kids choices."[64] Choice was encouraged by the way that children elected to use the equipment; they could invent their own activities because the play environment was suited to a wide variety of interpretations, requiring children's imagination to complete the picture.

PARKS COUNCIL ARCHIVES, DRAWINGS AND ARCHIVES COLLECTION OF THE AVERY ARCHITECTURAL AND FINE ARTS LIBRARY, COLUMBIA UNIVERSITY, IN THE CITY OF NEW YORK

Dattner discusses the design of the newly completed Adventure Playground, 1967.

Concentric concrete walls could become mazes, dungeons, or fortresses, and mounds could become volcanoes, igloos, or mountains. And of course children could invent other uses for the equipment that had not necessarily occurred to the designer. Reminiscent of Kahn's intentions for the Riverside Park playground proposal was Dattner's observation that the more general a form or object was at the playground, the more freedom it allowed children to impose their own meanings on it.

As he had at the Lauder cosmetics factory Dattner employed landforms at the playground to create topographic interest. A previously flat site was transformed into a topographically varied terrain that at the scale of a child presented a miniature world suggestive of hills, valleys, and plains. The geometrically derived abstracted landscape that he created was contemporaneous with the emerging field of earth art and was as much a work of sculpture as it was an example of architecture or landscape design. While the landforms provided a sculpted background for the children's activity, a large wooden pyramid placed in the center of the playground provided a focal counterpoint for the composition. With its squared sides the pyramid was the only element to be sited orthogonally in relation to Manhattan's street grid.: As the most architecturally defined element in the playground, the pyramid was linked to the design of the surrounding city, visible just outside the playground fence, thus encouraging children to imaginatively embrace the greater built environment as well.

The sculpted play equipment was tied together by serpentine concrete walls, reminiscent of Brazilian landscape architect Roberto Burle Marx's mazelike play area at Parque del Este in Caracas, Venezuela (from 1961).[65] The walls at the Adventure Playground facilitated Dattner's concept of continuous play as children could circulate around all the play equipment without ever touching the ground. The enclosing walls created a boundary between the hard-surfaced play area outside and the soft sandy area within, and the winding movement formed small intimate play recesses. Parents found the walls convenient for seating, allowing greater involvement and supervision than had been possible with the old benches that lined the playground perimeter. The varying heights of the walls were designed to accommodate different postures, like sitting, perching, and leaning. The serpentine walls were also specifically intended to support easels for children's art instruction, a programmatic aspect of the playground concurrent with Hoving's vision of the park as a setting for events. Likewise, the climbing poles, in addition to providing children with physical exercise, were located adjacent to amphitheater seating to provide a framework that could hold painted backdrops for children's performances in the playground. Art and craft

69

supplies, along with toys and books for storytelling, were stored with the play panels inside the wooden pyramid. (The resemblance of this structure to an ancient pyramid took on even greater significance to children when they learned that it contained a concealed chamber.)

The colors and textures of the playground were provided by the materials used in the playground's construction: granite block, concrete, wood, and sand. These muted natural tones, combined with the playground's mature trees, were intended to provide minimal visual discord with the surrounding park landscape. The lack of painted color also had a programmatic role: to provide a blank canvas for children's imaginations, allowing them to reinvent the playground according to their whims. Children were also quite literally encouraged to draw on the concrete forms with colored chalk under supervision of the playground supervisor. Color in the Adventure Playground became a fluid, adventure-promoting medium to be manipulated by children. The seemingly colorless playground embraced a modernist notion of process in art whereby color would be provided by children's imaginations, their art projects, and children themselves as they scrambled about the playground in variously colored clothing playing with brightly colored toys.

The Adventure Playground was a critical and popular success, and through awards, press, publications, and media attention it emerged as the single most famous playground in America, a must-see design for sociologists, educators, designers, and parents. Shortly after the playground opened, *The New York Times* announced: "The current mecca for visiting mothers and children is the Adventure Playground at 67th Street and Central Park West, just inside the park. On a recent sunny afternoon, mothers—and some fathers—were crowding the concrete steps leading down to the big sand pit where their children swarmed in continuous motion over the various play structures."[66]

The playground received numerous honors and awards, including citations from the Park Association of New York City, *Industrial Design* magazine, and the New York Chapter of the American Institute of Architects, which also singled out Dattner's play panels for an Environments Award as an example of "well-designed objects in the city's environment."[67] The playground was praised in both popular and professional press: Besides newspaper stories the playground appeared in *Life, Look, Newsweek, The New Yorker,* and *House and Garden* magazines, and it was featured in architectural, art, and design journals including such European publications as the French *L'Architecture d'Aujourd'hui* and the German *Bauwelt*.[68] The playground design revolution sparked a brief publishing frenzy from the late 1960s through the mid-1970s, and the Adventure Playground was represented in practically every publication on the subject, including foreign books in which Dattner's design, along with Friedberg's work, was portrayed as America's premier contribution to playground design. The "play" at the Adventure Playground was documented on film and became familiar to those who specialized in the design of public space as well as to the general public: The late urban sociologist William "Holly" Whyte recorded children at play there in his documentary films on urban open space, and the playground reached a far wider audience as children around the world watched the daily opening sequence for television's Sesame Street filmed on location at the playground.

The End of the Playground Revolution

The progressive playgrounds that had been pioneered by Noguchi and brought to fruition by Friedberg and Dattner gradually became park standards, as *The New York Times* noted in 1972: "In the last six years, the New Left of playground designers has practically become the establishment. Championed by parents, encouraged by a few far-seeing city officials, and under-written by foundations, the designers have created concrete mounds and soaring wooden structures that are steadily replacing or augmenting the old swing-and-seesaw playgrounds."[69] Although Dattner still believed that his original concept had been compromised by the prohibition of European-style adventure-play materials, the Adventure Playground was to be the closest that any designer would come to realizing a true adventure-type play experience in a city park.

Dattner designed four more privately sponsored playgrounds for Central Park in which he attempted to refresh his original playground design with different themes and geometric configurations. One of his later playgrounds was known as the Ancient Play Garden because the play equipment was based on abstracted elements of ancient Egyptian architecture from the collection of the neighboring Metropolitan Museum of Art. At the playground's opening in 1972 city parks administrator August Heckscher, whose grandfather had founded the Heckscher Playground in Central Park, noted that "for the first time, such a facility takes a historic theme as its base in blending education and enjoyment."[70] Other designers were commissioned to create unique playgrounds for Central Park through the 1970s, and this tradition continued into the 1980s under the administration of the Central Park Conservancy, spearheaded by Central Park Administrator Elizabeth Barlow Rogers. Notable playgrounds commissioned by the Conservancy included designs by landscape architects Paul Friedberg and Bruce Kelly. Friedberg's Rustic Playground, a witty homage to Olmsted and Vaux's vocabulary of park furnishings and landscape design elements, featured the park's most popular slide—cut directly into a natural rock outcropping. Bruce Kelly designed two playgrounds for the Conservancy that were a deliberate tribute to the distilled-classical styling, representational sculpture, and steel play equipment of park design from the Moses administration.

The era of playgrounds that were custom designed by artists, architects, and landscape architects effectively came to an end by the late 1980s because of increased concerns about liability for children's safety, a development that was directly related to the industrial standardization of play equipment. The innovative interlinked play structures pioneered by Dattner and Friedberg had been standardized into modular units by playground-equipment manufacturers. Dattner and Friedberg had themselves helped to pave the way for a return to commercial standardization through Dattner's experiments with portable modular Play Cubes and, more consequentially, through Friedberg's contracts with play-equipment manufacturers for prefabricated playground kits.[71] Play-equipment manufacturers established safety guidelines, recommended by children's safety experts, which dictated materials, heights, slopes, and railings for safe play. Because these companies accepted limited liability for playground accidents the play equipment was intentionally designed to restrict children's play activities to a set of prescribed routines that were judged to be safe. Municipalities became increasingly loathe to accept additional liability for custom-designed experimental—and potentially unsafe—equipment.

70

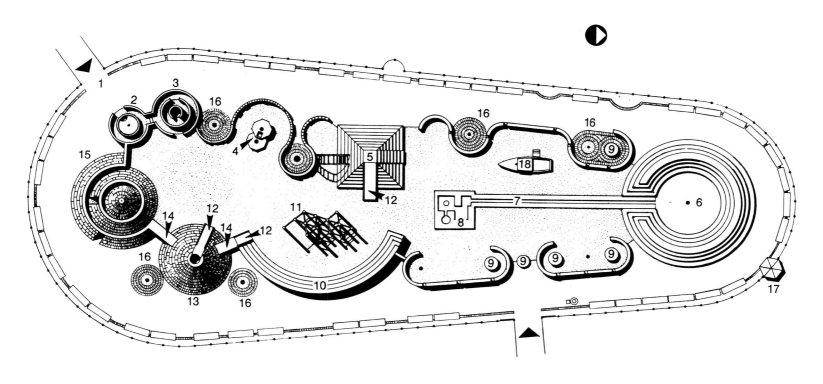

Plan of the Adventure Playground in Central Park, 1966	1	Entrance	5	Pyramid	9	Table	13	Volcano	16	Tree Pit
	2	Entrance Tower	6	Splashing Pool	10	Amphitheater	14	Tunnel	17	Tool Shed
	3	Maze	7	Water Channel	11	Climbing Poles	15	Concentric Mounds	18	Boat
	4	Tree Houses	8	Wading Pools	12	Slide		(Crater)		(not installed)

COURTESY OF RICHARD DATTNER

Virtually all playgrounds now constructed in New York City, as well as in most other American municipalities, are slight variations of standardized modular equipment offered by a handful of companies.

Preservation Issues

By 1990 Central Park possessed a comprehensive collection of playgrounds that represented distinct eras of designing for children's play, including Olmsted and Vaux's original Play Ground, intact examples of early Moses-era playgrounds, 1950s novelty playgrounds with rocketship and stagecoach play equipment, the Adventure Playground and its progeny from the 1960s, 1970s wooden frontiertown or fortress playgrounds, and the revival-themed playground designs from the 1980s. Most of these playgrounds required some degree of restoration work because of neglected maintenance as well as years of general wear and tear. The problem, of course, was that none of the playgrounds met current safety guidelines, and it was difficult, if not impossible, to bring them into compliance while retaining historic design integrity. But another problem—pertinent to all park furnishings and elements added to Central Park over the last century and a half—was whether to interpret the playgrounds as historical artifacts of landscape design, worthy of mandated preservation and protection.

The Central Park Conservancy, a private nonprofit organization, had assumed an increasingly greater role for the park's administration and restoration since the founding of the organization in 1980. The Conservancy had decided that playgrounds were distinct elements, separate from the historic Central Park landscape, which had changed over time and would continue to change: "Playgrounds should never be landmarked because they are above all about use and safety."[72] The Landmarks Preservation Commission of the City of New York, which has jurisdiction over all proposed changes to the Central Park Scenic Landmark, concurred with the Conservancy, and henceforth all changes to park playgrounds were reviewed by Landmarks staff without the customary public review mandated by New York City landmarks law. It was understood that so long as proposed changes to playgrounds did not alter the original boundaries of the playground, and therefore did not encroach upon the historic park, all changes would be approved de facto.

Throughout the 1990s the Central Park Conservancy, which had earlier commissioned new playgrounds by landscape architects Paul Friedberg and Bruce Kelly, systematically renovated and rebuilt park playgrounds through the Conservancy's Office of Landscape Architecture. All of the Moses-era playgrounds were completely rebuilt with new equipment that complied with guidelines for safe play. Additionally, all of the novelty play equipment was removed, and some of the 1970s wooden fortress playgrounds were modified or demolished. A few Central Park playgrounds that were deemed superfluous were removed entirely and replaced with lawn and shrubs. The five playgrounds designed by Richard Dattner met varying fates. While Dattner's Ancient Play Garden was carefully renovated by the Conservancy, preserving the original equipment, some of his other designs were completely demolished, and the remaining ones languished in peril. These deliberately neglected playgrounds remain endangered today. The high cost of concrete removal was the major obstacle to demolishing and rebuilding these playgrounds, and it is largely for this reason that many of them survived at all.

A play supervisor at the Adventure Playground assists children with modular play panels, 1967; splashing pool, water channel, and serpentine walls are visible in background.

PHOTO BY RICHARD DATTNER

The Central Park Conservancy Preservation Strategy

The Central Park Adventure Playground came under particular scrutiny in 1995 as part of a campaign to completely restore and rebuild Central Park's west-side perimeter landscape by the year 2000. Other modern landscape designs in Central Park had already caused considerable debate within the Conservancy about preservation issues, notably the Bolivar Plaza (located at the southern entrance to the park at Avenue of the Americas), which was ultimately magnificently restored to Gilmore D. Clarke's original bold mid-1950s classical-modernist design. The Adventure Playground generated similar aesthetically oriented preservation issues about validating frankly modern design within the pastoral park, with the added problem of recent safety guidelines for children's play. Almost thirty years after the playground had opened to laudatory press, the Conservancy had largely forgotten the playground's historical importance; indeed, it no longer called the playground by its correct name, referring to it instead as simply "the West 67th Street Playground."[73] The unique

programmatic concerns of the original playground and the integrity of its Brutalist aesthetics were lost on a generation of landscape architects and park administrators at the Conservancy who were steeped in the policies of historic revivalism. Committed to restoring what it perceived to be the Olmsted and Vaux style of landscape design, the Conservancy espoused a vague historically mimetic approach to landscape restoration.

The original programmatic initiatives of the Adventure Playground were restricted and ignored by the Conservancy's park administration. The annual neighborhood fundraising to hire a play supervisor ended before the Conservancy's Playground Partners took over playground maintenance in Central Park. As neighborhood residents changed over time the legacy of the unique characteristics of the playground were not always passed along to subsequent generations of parents. By discontinuing such original programmatic elements as art instruction and storytelling the community gradually lost stewardship for the original design. The Conservancy closed the tunnels inside the Adventure Playground, and some of the original safety features disappeared through neglected maintenance, including railings and gunwales on the slides. Chipped cement and rotted wood remained unrepaired. Art supplies, books, toys, and play panels moldered unused inside the pyramid, which was rarely opened. Rather than simply repair the playground the Conservancy decided to demolish it as part of a restored perimeter landscape. However, the water feature remained one of the most popular play features in the park, and anticipating public outcry should it be destroyed, the Conservancy decided to retain the feature in the new design. Assuming that it could raise the funds to remove the concrete sculpted play equipment, the Conservancy proposed cutting the playground in half, retaining the water feature in the northern end of the playground, and replacing the rest of the design with standard playground equipment, completely violating the interconnectedness of the original design. The Conservancy justified the radical plan as a concession to perceptions about safe play as well as to concerns about high maintenance costs generated by the large expanse of sand, an ironic echo of Dattner's optimistic observation from thirty years earlier: "There is no question that these playgrounds will be more expensive to maintain, but playgrounds can't be built anymore for maintenance men."[74] Maintenance had again become a chief concern dictating playground design in Central Park.

At the Conservancy's Office of Landscape Architecture the plan to demolish half the playground prompted a lively in-house debate about the playground's integrity as a work of landscape design. In an attempt to get some cursory feedback from playground parents the Conservancy sponsored an informal playground survey as well as some invitation-only meetings with neighborhood parents (who happened to be donors to the Conservancy). The survey revealed that parents were actually comfortable with the Adventure Playground, and the meetings demonstrated community respect for the playground design. After becoming reacquainted with the playground's history, the Conservancy eventually adopted what it considered to be a preservation strategy for the entire playground, despite conflicting opinions about its design merit. As a concession to maintenance concerns a compromise was agreed upon to greatly reduce the sand area and to separate it from the water channel where children were mixing sand with water and clogging the drains. Because retrofitting Dattner's custom-designed equipment to meet safety guidelines proved

PHOTOGRAPHER UNKNOWN

Pyramid, 1967

PHOTO BY NORMAN MCGRATH

View of playground from atop the Pyramid, 1967

PHOTOGRAPHER UNKNOWN

Splashing pool, 1967

PHOTO BY NORMAN MCGRATH

Concentric mounds, tunnel, and volcano, 1967

The Adventure Playground after renovation, 1997: Note that the sand has been replaced by safety surface and new wooden play features are smaller than the old.

impossible, it was decided that the old equipment could be "grandfathered" so long as it was not significantly altered. This permitted the Conservancy the latitude to creatively upgrade safety at the playground, including a new poured-in-place safety surface to replace the existing asphalt and discrete railings added at precipitous heights. However, any equipment that required significant rebuilding, including the rotted wood of the tree house, climbing bars, and pyramid, would have to be removed entirely and replaced according to safety guidelines. The question then became whether to reproduce modified versions of the original equipment or to replace them with something entirely new. Ultimately, this decision was based on criteria that were unrelated to preservation or safety and was instead dictated by the murky policies that govern private donations to a public park.

The Central Park Conservancy relies primarily on private donations to pay for its myriad functions including administration, education, training, design, and maintenance. In order to fund landscape projects donors are courted with the promise of some type of lasting acknowledgment for their philanthropic gift. Usually a plaque will suffice to note the gift, but sometimes donors are lured with the promise of their name on a garden, a bench, or perhaps a building. This strategy is hardly new to Central Park as evidenced by the philanthropic gift of the Heckscher Playground in 1926, and it actually became a staple of the Moses administration in the 1950s to secure funding for park projects after federal work-relief programs ended. Today Central Park contains a great variety of statues, benches, gardens, recreational facilities, buildings, and playgrounds named after the legions of private donors who paid for them. The Adventure Playground, however, presented the unique problem of enticing a donor to restore a design feature that had, just thirty years earlier, already been donated and acknowledged. In other words, if the playground was to be strictly restored to its prior condition and original name, then there might appear to be no product to have justified the donor's considerable investment. The Conservancy therefore decided that adding a new feature to the playground would provide the donor with a tangible product for the monetary gift.

The Conservancy considered a variety of new design features that could be added to the playground and yet be consistent with a preservation-minded renovation, including the restoration of an original design element that had never been constructed (a small boat that was to have been sited alongside the water

channel) and the resurrection of a flagpole that had long been missing from the playground fort. Adding a new color scheme to the playground was also considered. This would have violated the intentionally neutral color scheme of the original design—the natural hues of the sand, trees, granite block, and concrete found in the playground. In an attempt to adapt a historical feature of the playground for a new use ideas for new colors were derived from the "supergraphics" patterns that had been painted on the original play panels. The most important task was to find a new vertical element to replace the wood pyramid, formerly the focus of the playground. Because the pyramid required substantial rebuilding, its removal provided the opportunity to replace it with a new piece of equipment at the most prominent site in the playground. The decision to replace the pyramid essentially opened the possibility of adding a new sculpture to the park, albeit as play equipment: a rare and enticing prospect for a donor to Central Park. "The Central Park Conservancy felt the pyramid was too steep in its present form," noted Dattner at the time. "So I suggested making it lower. But they wanted something new. They have a donor, and he wants to make a new statement." [75]

The controversial renovation plan was highlighted in a *New York Times* article that appeared on the front page of the weekly design section. The article, which was about preserving modern landscape architecture, noted the potentially "sticky donor issues" connected with courting private money to restore a public playground.[76] However, the renovation plan received little public reaction until a sign went up at the playground noting the pending construction. In circumstances similar to the Battle of Central Park forty years earlier one of the mothers who had been part of the coalition that built the original Adventure Playground was taking her dog for a walk in the vicinity of the playground when she noticed the sign. This was the first that she had heard of the playground reconstruction, and she alerted her neighbors, including several members of the original Committee for a Creative Playground who still lived in the neighborhood. Dedicated to ensuring a historically appropriate renovation, the neighbors formed a new organization called Friends of the Adventure Playground, under the aegis of LANDMARK WEST!, an Upper West Side preservation organization. Neighborhood parents signed petitions, attended meetings, and lobbied politicians and park officials in an effort to stop the project and redirect the playground renovation along historic preservation guidelines.

Friends of the Adventure Playground drafted a scope-of-work for the entire playground, outlining strategies to resolve preservation and safe-play issues for all aspects of the design. Disregarding the venerable history of community opposition to controversial park proposals, the Conservancy held steadfastly to its plan and refused to accommodate suggestions by the neighborhood group. The Conservancy's conduct raised questions about the accountability of a private nonprofit organization that dictates design policy for public property. A deadlock between the community and the Conservancy ensued, and *The New York Times* noted the "increasingly contentious meetings with playground users and community members" at which participants voted overwhelmingly against the Conservancy's proposal.[77] Friends of the Adventure Playground decided to consult the playground's original architect for guidance about how to resolve the issue, and in a process similar to the creation of the original playground Dattner held a design meeting with concerned parents at which they could air their feelings about playground safety, maintenance, and historic integrity. Parents' suggestions for improving the renovation plan were transformed into design proposals by Dattner, for example, an adaptation of the pyramid to accommodate different lengths of slides for children of varying ages.

Pressure came from past and present park donors, local politicians, state senators, and even the United States Department of the Interior. The New York City Parks Department, which retained ultimate jurisdiction over Central Park, was perhaps the most persuasive organization to enter the fray; it was headed by Commissioner Henry Stern, who had served as executive director under Hoving's parks administration at the time the Adventure Playground was originally built. The Conservancy finally capitulated to community demands to preserve the Adventure Playground, and a compromise plan was developed whereby the Conservancy agreed to consult with Dattner about any changes to the playground design. The final renovation plan preserved the original playground design but proposed rebuilding the wooden play elements at lower heights in accordance with safety guidelines. The wooden elements, which had formerly been the vertical foci in the playground's landscape of concrete and granite block would now be dwarfed by the masonry elements. Some of the original equipment was retrofitted with railings, and the entire playground was repaved with a poured-in-place safety surface. The major, and perhaps most damaging, change to the original design integrity was the decision to restrict the broad expanse of sand to a smaller, more contained area, a change that greatly altered the appearance and programmatic intent of the playground design. Although the playground was significantly compromised through design changes wrought by the renovation, the Brutalist-style hardscape elements of the original landscape design—which would have been the most difficult features to replicate had they been lost—were entirely retained and repaired. The playground reconstruction commenced in the fall of 1996, and the Adventure Playground officially reopened on June 24, 1997, with a gala party given by business-media mogul Michael Bloomberg, the donor who funded the playground renovation. The name "Adventure Playground" was officially inscribed in the fence at the entrance to the playground; a new plaque acknowledged the donor's gift. The reconstructed playground remains one of the most popular children's play areas in Central Park.

Conclusion

The Central Park Adventure Playground was a pivotal work of landscape design and survives as perhaps the most important extant modern playground in America. The Adventure Playground reinterpreted postwar European concepts of adventure play, combined with emerging theories about the importance of children's play, into a uniquely American conception based on observations of how children carved out recreation space in the somewhat forbidding environment of New York City. The playground is also significant as the distillation and culmination of a rich history of precedents by progressive designers to transform the American playground from a fenced-in plot containing disparate play equipment into a sculpturally integrated play environment. Some of these pioneering playground designs were the work of the most famous and revered of modern designers, including Isamu Noguchi and Louis Kahn, whose plans, models, and sketches have been extensively represented

in catalogs and museum retrospectives, while the work of other designers who contributed to the legacy of modern playground design, like Albert Mayer and Julian Whittelsey, has been less well documented and deserves reevaluation. Almost all of the important postwar experiments in designing for children's play occurred in New York City, and the evidence of this era is housed in various city archives and documented in architectural journals from that period; the actual playgrounds from this era rarely survive.

The lack of playground preservation in New York City is not only a direct result of increased concern for children's safety and liability constraints but also reflects a narrow interpretation of historic landscape integrity by both landscape and preservation professionals. New York City is certainly not unique in this regard. Most municipalities seem unwilling to view their parks as compilations of landscape contributions from a variety of eras. Instead, they decide on a specific period of significance and attempt to restore their parks to that era, destroying actual historic artifacts from later eras and replacing them with semblances of earlier ones. Frequently park furnishings, including buildings and sculpture, are considered ancillary to the park landscape and receive no consideration whatsoever from preservationists. This restrictive view of landscape preservation is, unfortunately, the prevalent attitude at most city, state, and federal preservation projects, and artifacts and designs from the recent past are those most likely to be discarded.

Not only are preservationists ill-equipped to deal with multiple extant layers of park history, but they are also loathe to recognize relatively recent types of landscape design. Preservationists and landscape architects must acknowledge new categories of landscape design—including playgrounds—that have emerged during the modern era as valid expressions of landscape art, worthy of consideration for preservation. A rich history of American landscape design exists outside the confines of the traditional preservationist's purview of park, garden, or scenic roadway. Some of these recent landscape categories include playgrounds, urban plazas, shopping centers, and corporate campuses. Such landscapes are sorely lacking preservation constituents and, as has been shown by the history of playground design, are particularly vulnerable to modification and removal. The preservation of the Adventure Playground in Central Park is a unique example of particularly dedicated park preservationists and concerned neighborhood residents who recognized the historical importance of the playground design and were willing to fight for its survival. Such scenarios are rare and unlikely to be repeated as we witness the disappearance of modern playground designs and the concurrent diminution of a considerable legacy of modern landscape architecture from the American landscape at the end of the twentieth century.

Michael Owen Gotkin works as a landscape architect and city planner and has been an advocate for the preservation of postwar architecture in New York City. In addition to design and planning for the Central Park Conservancy he has organized exhibitions for the Cooper-Hewitt National Design Museum and is currently preparing an exhibition and book about the aesthetics and politics of playground architecture.

1 Recent years have witnessed the demolition and modification of many historic sites for children's play and amusement in Central Park, including the children's pony-riding loop, the Central Park Children's Zoo, and numerous playgrounds from different eras.

2 Although the Great Lawn was significantly altered in a recent reconstruction, the integrity of the ovoid lawn design, as well as its scenic relation to the small pond, was retained in the new design; thus, the alteration of this notable landscape element escaped substantial controversy.

3 Galen Cranz, *The Politics of Park Design: A History of Urban Parks in America* (Cambridge: MIT Press, 1982), 87. See also Roy Rosenzweig and Elizabeth Blackmar, *The Park and the People: A History of Central Park* (New York: Cornell University Press, 1992), 392-95.

4 Ibid., 395.

5 Ibid., 451.

6 Robert Moses, "Municipal Recreation," *American Architect and Architecture* (November 1936), 22. See also "Playground Design and Equipment," *Architectural Forum* (October 1943), 140.

7 Lady Allen of Hurtwood, *Planning for Play* (London: Oxford University Press, 1968), 55.

8 Alfred Ledermann and Alfred Trachsel, *Creative Playgrounds and Recreation Centers* (New York: Frederick A. Praeger, 1968), 110-13. See also Avrid Bengtsson, *Adventure Playgrounds* (London: Granada, 1972).

9 Lady Allen of Hurtwood, *Planning for Play*, 62.

10 Isamu Noguchi, *The Isamu Noguchi Garden Museum* (New York: Harry N. Abrams, 1987), 143.

11 Jay Jacobs, "Projects for Playgrounds," *Art in America* (November/December 1967), 45.

12 Isamu Noguchi, *A Sculptor's World* (New York: Harper & Row, 1968), 22.

13 Noguchi, *The Isamu Noguchi Garden Museum*, 144.

14 Noguchi alleged that an assistant to Robert Moses, Mr. Mulholland, had practically challenged him to create an accident-free playground and had offered some encouragement that the Contoured Playground proposal might be tested in Central Park. See Noguchi, *A Sculptor's World*, 24-25, and *The Isamu Noguchi Garden Museum*, 150.

15 Jacobs, "Projects for Playgrounds," 39. See also "Approve Final Plan for Disputed U.N. Playground," *Architectural Record* (October 1952), 22, 366; "Playgrounds Have Discovered Design," *Architectural Record* (January 1954), 157; Noguchi, *The Isamu Noguchi Garden Museum*, 152.

16 "Approve Final Plan for Disputed U.N. Playground," *Architectural Record*, 366; "Model of Sculptor's Playground Rejected by Moses Is on View," *The New York Herald Tribune* (March 23, 1952).

17 The once ubiquitous sight of painted steel play equipment designed to resemble fantastical images from children's fairy tales, science fiction, and the Wild West has all but disappeared from New York City. The last vestiges of postwar novelty play equipment were only recently erased from the Central Park landscape with the removal of the West 76th Street Playground in 1995.

18 Correspondence dated May 14, 1959, from Executive Officer of The City of New York Department of Parks (signatory on letter unknown; signature illegible) to Frank Caplan, President, Creative Playthings, Inc., collection of Lily Auchincloss Architecture & Design Study Center, Museum of Modern Art, New York.

19 Correspondence dated May 18, 1959, from Frank Caplan to Greta Daniels, associate curator, Museum of Modern Art, collection of Lily Auchincloss Architecture & Design Study Center, Museum of Modern Art, New York.

20 Jacobs, "Projects for Playgrounds," 50.

21 Ibid.

22 Lady Allen of Hurtwood, quoted in Charles L. Mee, Jr., "Putting the Play in Playgrounds," *New York Times Magazine* (November 6, 1966), 116.

23 The Council for Parks and Playgrounds and the Park Association of New York City were later merged into one organization, the Parks Council. The Parks Council Archive, now part of the Drawings Collection of the Avery Architectural and Fine Arts Library, Columbia University, is an invaluable collection of texts, correspondence, drawings, photographs, and films related to parks and playgrounds in New York City. The Parks Council Archive preserves what was once a great legacy of advocacy for children's play environments.

24 The Park Association of New York City, *New Ideas for City Playgrounds* (New York: The Park Association of New York City, 1964), collection of Parks Council Archive, Drawings Collection of the Avery Architectural and Fine Arts Library, Columbia University.

25 Murray Illson, "Playground Design Exhibition Given Cool Reception by Morris," *The New York Times* (February 17, 1964).

26 Park Association of New York City, *New Ideas for City Playgrounds*.

27 "Community Playground Facilities," *The Playground Revolution* (New York: Park Association, 1966).

28 "Harlem's Playful Playground," *Architectural Forum* (March 1961), 106; "Franklin Plaza: new life for an urban complex," *Architectural Record* (July 1965), 170. Franklin Plaza was later converted to a private cooperative; the landscaped plaza, including the custom-designed details by Mayer, is intact and well-cared for.

29 "Making Public Housing Human," *Progressive Architecture* (January 1965), 177.

30 Ibid., 178. The plaza at Carver Houses is intact, but extremely dilapidated.

31 "Designing the Spaces In Between," *Architectural Record* (March 1968), 121.

32 Henry Raymont, "Two Top Architects Get a Hoving Bid," *The New York Times* (October 6, 1966), 49.

33 John McPhee "A Roomful of Hovings," *The New Yorker* (May 20, 1967).

34 Ada Louise Huxtable, "New Era for Parks: Hoving and Young Appointees Hope to Scrap the Traditional and Try the New," *The New York Times* (February 10, 1966), 50.

35 Raymont, "Two Top Architects Get a Hoving Bid," 49.

36 *The New York Times Magazine* (July 10, 1966), 15.

37 Ralph Blumenthal, "Hoving Planning Park Food Kiosks," *The New York Times* (February 10, 1966), 39.

38 Weintraub, 11, 15.

39 "Parks and Recreation" [white paper / policy statement authored by Thomas Hoving and issued by John V. Lindsay, Fusion Candidate for Mayor] (October 8, 1965), Parks Council Archive, Drawings Collection of the Avery Architectural and Fine Arts Library, Columbia University, New York.

40 Ibid.

41 Robert Caro, *The Power Broker: Robert Moses and the Fall of New York* (New York: A.A. Knopf, 1974), 984-1004.

42 Leonard Lauder, quoted in Douglas E. Kneeland, "City Accepts 'Adventure' Playground in Central Park," *The New York Times* (June 9, 1966).

43 Jacobs, "Projects for Playgrounds," *Art in America*, 39.

44 John Morris Dixon, "Streamlined Factory: White Streak Along the Open Road," *Architectural Forum* (March 1967), 76-83.

45 Richard Dattner, "Playgrounds Aren't for Playing; Playgrounds Are for Growing and Learning," *American School Board Journal* (April 1973), 30.

46 Richard Dattner, *Design for Play* (New York: Van Nostrand Reinhold, 1969), 15.

47 Elisabeth Kendall Thompson, "Recreation: A Chance for Innovative Design," *Architectural Record* (August 1967), 120.

48 McCandlish Phillips, "How to Put Play in Playgrounds," *The New York Times* (October 6, 1966), 49.

49 Dattner, *Design for Play*, 66.

50 Arthur Rosenblatt, "Open Space Design: New York shows how in its park program," *Architectural Record* (August 1967), 110.

51 Mary Burt Baldwin, "Childhood Occupations . . . given glorious stimulation in the new Adventure Playground in Manhattan's Central Park," *Chicago Tribune* (June 5, 1967).

52 Dattner, *Design for Play*, 47-48.

53 Ibid., 75. For a description of a play supervisor at work in the Adventure Playground, see "Talk of the Town—Playground," *The New Yorker* (August 22, 1972), 30.

54 "Work Is Ready to Start On 'Adventure Playground,'" *West Side News and Morningsider* (September 29, 1966), 8.

55 Ibid., 68.

56 David M. Grant, "With a Hop, Skip and Jump, Playgrounds Go Modern," *The New York Times* (June 17, 1973), H-8.

57 Dattner, *Design for Play*, 38.

58 "On Making a Playground Swing," *American School & University Magazine* (August 1971), 19.

59 For "play parks" see Lady Allen of Hurtwood, *Planning for Play,* 85-104.

60 Brownlee and DeLong, *Louis I. Kahn*, 112.

61 "Dattner, "Playgrounds Aren't for Playing, Playgrounds are for Growing and Learning," 31.

62 Tom McMorrow, "Playground for the Future is Fun Now," *New York Daily News* (August 27, 1967), B-1.

63 "Playgrounds: Design or Happening?" *Architectural & Engineering News* (September 1967), 59.

64 Grant, "With a Hop, Skip and Jump, Playgrounds Go Modern," H-8.

65 Anthony Walmsley, "South America: Appraisal of a Master Artist," *Landscape Architecture* (July 1963), 265.

66 Lisa Hammel, "Playing is More Than Just Fun and Games," *The New York Times* (August 14, 1967), 38.

67 Franklin Whitehouse, "Bleakness of the City Need Not Be Destiny: Architects Discover Some Bright Spots," *The New York Times* (January 12, 1969), H-1, 4.

68 European articles include "'Parcours d'Aventures' pour Enfants, Central Park," *L'Architecture d'Aujourd'hui* (Avril-Mai 1967), 99, 103; "Abenteurspielplatz im Central Park von New York," *Bauwelt* (January 1970), 42; "Cinq Aires de Jeux: New York," *L'Architecture d'Aujourd'hui* (Fevrier-Mars 1971), 72.

69 Lisa Hammel, "Two Playground Designers Who Used to Be 'Rebels,'" *The New York Times* (November 29, 1972), 38.

70 "A Historic Theme for New Park," *New York Post,*(November 30, 1972), 23; see also Barbara Allen Guilfoyle, "Sand Castles," *Industrial Design* (October 1973), 33-37.

71 For Dattner's Play Cubes, see Nan Ickeringill, "An Instant Kind of Playground," *The New York Times* (May 20, 1969), 36; "Play's the Thing," *Architectural Forum* (June 1969), 17. For

Friedberg's prefabricated playgrounds see Mee, "Putting the Play in Playgrounds," 120.

72 A senior landscape architect at the Conservancy was so quoted in Lincoln Anderson, "Adventure Playground Friends Win Key Support in 67th Street Fight," *The Westsider* (July 18-24, 1996), 16. The Conservancy's preservation policies are outlined in Elizabeth Barlow Rogers, *Rebuilding Central Park: A Management and Restoration Plan* (Cambridge: MIT Press, 1987). For the Conservancy's agreement with the New York City Landmarks Commission about retrofitting playgrounds, see the New York City Landmarks Preservation Commission, Docket #97/0845, Staff/Commission Report #96-0036, "West 67th Street Playground and Adjacent Landscape," October 11, 1995.

73 Information in this paper concerning the Central Park Conservancy's role in renovating the Adventure Playground is based on the author's employment at the Conservancy's Office of Landscape Architecture and his intimate involvement with this project, as well as other Central Park landscape renovation projects. All images and documents pertaining to the playground renovation that were consulted for this paper are part of a collection owned by the author.

74 Mee, "Putting the Play in Playgrounds, 119.

75 Anne Raver, "Cherishing Landscapes As Living Art," *The New York Times* (November 30, 1995), C-6.

76 Ibid.

77 Janet Allon, "Adventure vs. Safety in Playground Renovation Battle," *The New York Times* (June 23, 1996), CY-6.

The Garden Conservancy:
Lessons from the First Decade
John Fitzpatrick

Visitors to the Ruth Bancroft Garden at Walnut Creek, California, enter through a fanciful pavilionlike structure.

The Garden Conservancy was founded in 1989 to preserve exceptional American gardens. The idea was to establish an organization that would be a resource for private owners of exceptional gardens who wished to turn their creations into public gardens. The Conservancy's role was seen as assisting in the establishment of local nonprofit ownership and operation of gardens of national significance. Much of the young organization's success has been due to its ability to respond to unanticipated opportunities with effective strategies.

Since its beginning the Conservancy has assisted a broad range of gardens, including several that were already in nonprofit or public ownership but in need of a helping hand. Although there is no essential difference between the way we treat gardens less than fifty years old and those that are older, some different issues do arise. The work the Conservancy does with projects can be divided into five main categories: documenting the garden, securing the future of the site, building support, developing a vision, and managing resources. Documenting can include anything from photographs and plant lists to full site maps of plants and other features, oral histories, garden archaeology, collections of archival images and written records, histories, and conditions surveys. Securing the future of the site includes such legal arrangements as deeding a property to a nonprofit organization, preparing a conservation easement (which might be held by the Conservancy), securing an endowment for the garden's operation, or applying for listing in the state and national historic registers. Building support is about fund-raising and team-building—finding volunteers, board members, donors, and professional staff. Developing a vision includes goal-setting and defining the organization's mission—developing both the intuitive, unspoken dreams as well as the master plans and strategic plans that organizations require. Managing the resources is about the effective use of money, information, and human resources to move an organization toward fulfillment of its goals.

When a request for sponsorship comes in we ask the owners to complete a garden survey and to provide other supporting materials. These materials are circulated to our professional screening committee. When it appears that a property meets criteria of significance and feasibility, representatives of the screening committee visit the garden and meet with the key individuals. The screening committee's recommendation is taken to the Conservancy's board of directors, which makes a decision about further action.

Conservancy staff does not respond to new projects with a set plan for priorities and action. Preservation plans and a working relationship are developed in response to each garden's unique circumstances—its assets, significant features, problems, condition, goals, and mission. The Garden Conservancy may provide anything from endorsement or technical assistance to a partnership or direct management of operations.

Gardens we have worked with that were designed in the last fifty years include the Ruth Bancroft Garden at Walnut Creek, California; the Humes Japanese Stroll Garden at Mill Neck, New York; and the James Rose residence in Ridgewood, New Jersey. The Conservancy's newest project is the garden of Emmott and Ione Chase of Orting, Washington.

The Ruth Bancroft Garden was the Conservancy's first project; it provides the most complete case study of what we do. The garden was started by Ruth Bancroft in 1972 as a 2.5-acre garden of curvilinear island beds laid out by the late California plantsman and garden designer Lester Hawkins. Bancroft planted the raised beds with her extensive collection of succulents, cacti, and other plants native to arid regions of the world.

Between 1989 and 1994 the Garden Conservancy played a leadership role in establishing the property as a public garden. The garden has been mapped and inventoried. A conservation easement on the property has been given to the Garden Conservancy. An oral history about the creation of the garden has been published. A nonprofit has been formed as a supporting organization of the Conservancy. An executive director has been hired. A volunteer program assists Bancroft in the garden as well as in leading tours and managing special events. A fund-raising plan is in operation. A master plan has been completed for the development of the site as a public garden. Bancroft has deeded four acres, including the original garden, to the supporting friends organization. It now operates the garden, and the Conservancy has one representative from the friends group on its board of directors.

The Humes Japanese Stroll Garden began as a two-acre garden on the North Shore estate of Ambassador and Mrs. John P. Humes in the early 1960s. It was laid out by Douglas deFaya, a Japanese-American landscape gardener, as a setting for an imported tea house. In 1981 Humes hired garden designer Stephen Morrell to rehabilitate the garden with the idea of opening it to the public. Morrell added a new entrance walk, a parking lot, a wisteria arbor, and other features, expanding the garden to four acres. Humes left the garden to the Humes Foundation at his death in 1985. The garden was opened to the public two years later, but in 1993, finding that it could not meet the operation's financial needs, the Humes Foundation decided to close the garden. Alerted to the potential loss of this significant public garden, the Garden Conservancy signed a short-term agreement to assume the management of the garden while long-term plans were developed. That agreement has continued, and in 1998 the Conservancy organized a capital campaign that led to the rehabilitation of the pond and waterfall—a central feature of the garden.

Work with the Humes Japanese Stroll Garden has been a matter of buying time by maintaining the garden and its basic public programs while rebuilding local support and exploring solutions for its future.

The steps winding down the hill at the Humes Japanese Stroll Garden represent a mountain stream flowing to the sea.

James Rose built a house and garden at Ridgewood, New Jersey, in 1953. As it was developed over the years the property became a masterpiece of modern landscape architecture. At Rose's death in 1991 the nonprofit corporation he had founded assumed possession of the property and began to realize his dream—the establishment of the James Rose Center for Landscape Architectural Research and Design.

The Conservancy formed a working partnership with the James Rose Center in 1993 to act as an advisor and advocate for the rehabilitation and operation of the property, organizing several one-day programs at the property to introduce Rose and his work to a wider public. The Center completed the preliminary application for listing the property in the state and national registers, and documentation of this property as well as other Rose designs is now well under way. Rehabilitation plans for the north end of the residence, Rose's studio and apartment, and adjacent garden spaces have been prepared. In 1994 we helped create an advisory council of local advocates for the property. They produced a site brochure and planned the Center's first fund-raising event in support of the rehabilitation work.

In September 1994 the Conservancy accepted a conservation easement on the 4.5-acre Chase property as a first step in its preservation. The garden's distinctive California-style design near the house—including two ornamental pools, an entrance courtyard, and a curvilinear concrete patio with fire pit—was completed by local landscape architect Rex Zumwalt in 1962. Ione Chase has added to the Zumwalt design by developing an alpine lawn on ground sloping away from the house and a woodland garden, largely of Northwest natives, under a stand of Douglas fir trees. Looking beyond the conservation easement and the documentation it required, the Conservancy has started working with local advocates to develop an organization that can assume the care and support of the garden in the future. The goal will be to establish the garden as an independent nonprofit operation, similar to the Bancroft Garden.

For almost a decade the Conservancy worked with a number of groups involved in preserving gardens. In all of these projects diverse teams have been assembled, including landscape historians, horticulturists, people who can give money, people who can raise money, newsletter writers, garden volunteers—in short, the whole range of people who can use a site and contribute to its

preservation. The Conservancy has learned how important it is to encourage emerging friends groups to tackle small projects appropriate to their resources. Meanwhile, the Conservancy develops long-term strategies. In all of these projects it is important to recognize that it is not sufficient to preserve the physical fabric of a garden; the local support groups must be built to carry these gardens into the future. Telling the stories of the gardens connects the people to the sites and builds teams.

A special aspect of preservation work with recent landscapes is that there are often surviving individuals who have intimate knowledge of the garden and its creation. This can either be a great help in documentation and building support for a garden or it can be an obstacle to the plans of the nonprofit owner. The Conservancy has found how difficult it can be to determine the level of significance for a site. While some gardens are quickly identified as nationally or locally significant, there are many others for which significance is difficult to assess. There seems to be more uncertainty in determining significance for landscapes less than fifty years old.

In such cases documentation, garden archaeology, and landscape reports do not always gain automatic support from the people outside preservation circles. The time and expense for such work needs to be justified to gain public support. As landscape preservationists we need to remind ourselves that cultural landscape reports are one step along the way, not the final product of preservation work. As useful as they are for planning and interpretation, they are tools for the work, not the work itself.

One thing that sets the Garden Conservancy apart from other preservation organizations is the fact that it was started by serious garden makers and horticulturists and continues to find its primary support among the garden-loving public. This means that the Conservancy is a new source of enthusiasm and expertise for landscape preservation. At the same time, many of the local supporters for Conservancy projects are unfamiliar with current preservation practices—and the planning process, options for treatment, interpretive plans, master plans, and maintenance plans on which professionals rely. Part of our work is "translating" the preservation process for local supporters and justifying it to ensure their continued participation.

In the view of the Garden Conservancy good gardeners are essential for good garden-preservation work. Gardeners have an expectation seldom found on preservation agendas—the expectation that preserved gardens will be fine public gardens, beautiful places for learning and spiritual renewal, and examples of responsible stewardship of ecosystems and genetic diversity. Helping gardeners fulfill such expectations in addition to preservation objectives is the Garden Conservancy's singular opportunity.

John Fitzpatrick is the former projects manager for the Garden Conservancy, Cold Spring, New York.

Epilogue:
Nourishing the Human Gene Pool:
Let Us Make and Preserve a
Legacy of Landscape Architecture
Richard Haag

In *The Decline of the West* (1926) Oswald Spengler writes of "the landscape without which life, thought, and soul are inconceivable." I confess that I have a near obsession to make landscapes—for it is through this creative art that the ego can be balanced by the altruism of the gift to society. Put another way, perhaps this drive to make gardens is a desire for connection with all of humankind, especially now, as we are drawn inexorably into more intense social (and now electronic) relationships that weaken the two-million-year-old relationship with a Nature in retreat. I hasten to add that it is as important to recognize a seminal contemporary landscape and to preserve it as it is to create it.

With this stated, I would like to recommend the following fifteen techniques for the preservation of contemporary landscapes:

I. Encourage the American Society of Landscape Architects (ASLA) to review and strengthen existing policies concerning the preservation of historic sites and designed projects of national significance with art commissions and other reviewing authorities. Additional recommended policies for preserving contemporary landscapes: establishing the eligibility of landscape architects for "one percent for art" programs and protecting properties of the mind, such as intellectual properties, copyrights, etcetera.

II. Encourage the ASLA to use its tax-exempt nonprofit status to set up an arm of its organization to serve as a project sponsor or "umbrella" for "Friends of the Landscape" to implement, extend, maintain, and preserve landscapes.

III. Proclaim pride of authorship: Sign works, publicize, become identified with the project.

IV. Put your work out there to be judged by your peers and the public through awards, competitions, publications, literature, and press releases—both local and national.

V. Write a retainer clause into significant contracts that are legally bound to the project rather than to the owner. Write in a value-added clause regarding subsequent sales with a percentage of the increased value remitted to the landscape architect.

VI. List or register (in the records at Wave Hill or in special permanent collections in university libraries) accurate as-built drawings, a statement of intent, management and preservation manuals, etcetera.

VII. Dedicate public landscapes as living memorials to prominent persons whose heirs will guard that legacy and perhaps contribute to maintaining it.

VIII. Set aside a particular landscape as a life estate, as a landscape conservancy that is tax abated or exempt in perpetuity.

IX. Apply "endangered species" law to protect contemporary landscapes.

Garden of Planes, 1991, Bloedel Reserve, Bainbridge Island, Washington

X. Apply restrictive laws to protect and preserve contemporary landscapes.

XI. Compile a national list of enabling laws, granting and funding agencies, private foundations, donors, etcetera. For example, as early as the 1960s Maryland offered tax abatement on particular properties.

XII. Reconstitute inheritance-tax laws with regard to exemplary landscapes. Tax notable landscapes at actual-use value rather than at the value of the highest potential developed use.

XIII. Check out architects as well as other countries (for example, the British National Trust) for different approaches to similar concerns.

XIV. Suggest that this symposium discuss these techniques and invent others. Give credit to this symposium for its focus.

XV. Befriend the groundskeeper.

I would now like to look at these proposals in the context of my own experience.

Garden of Planes, first garden in the Sequence of Gardens, Bloedel Reserve, Bainbridge Island, Washington (1986)

Bloedel, the owner/donor, began to bequeath his estate to the University of Washington. Before doing so, he held a limited competition to select a landscape architect to guide development. My firm was selected and continued in this role for seven years, completing a major project every year. One small but significant project was to convert the swimming pool into a landscape experience. The concept of the Garden of Planes was envisioned, drawn to scale, and presented to the design-review committee on site.

The hexagonal-shaped concrete plane surrounding the pool was sawn into squares and selected squares removed. The pool was filled with sand and the surface folded into seven planes forming two pyramids, one twenty-four feet by twenty-four feet inverted with a low point of minus four feet, the other sixteen by twenty-four feet with a ridge of plus three feet—all covered with moss except the remaining concrete squares. Although the eye observes only five planes, the mind solves the equation.

Mound Garden, 1964, Seattle Center, Seattle, Washington

Jordan Park, Everett, Washington, 1973

The plan was accepted with a few conditions: 1) no moss or lawn in openings in the concrete squares; 2) the tilted planes to be defined with metal dividers; 3) planes to be formed of crushed granite.

We dedicated the Garden of Planes to Professor Jay Appleton, English geographer and landscape theorist. Bloedel had supported Appleton's research on experiencing the landscape, and the garden was a tribute to Appleton's ultimate minimalism—the yin-yang of prospect and refuge.

Bloedel then reacquired the property from the university and endowed the Arbor Fund—a foundation to develop, maintain, and manage the reserve. This new committee retained a new landscape architect, who was instructed to redesign the Garden of Planes. Fortunately, the original garden was photographed along with the three other gardens of the Sequence of Gardens for submittal for an ASLA design award. The Sequence of Gardens includes the Reflection Pool, the Bird Sanctuary, the Anteroom, and the Garden of Planes. Together they received the Society's Presidential Award for Excellence in Design for 1986.

The Mound Garden, Seattle Center, Seattle, Washington (1963)

Lawrence Halprin, noted landscape architect, retained my office to supervise the construction of pools at the base of the Space Needle. The excavation contractor was hauling and dumping the soil into Lake Union and thus causing islands to pop up offshore. Not good. We reasoned with the contractor to stockpile the soil in barrows on a nearby site within the center. These tumuli became the Mound Garden. Was this an earthwork or what? It should be noted that the mounds preserved the half block from becoming a parking lot. In 1986 the City leased the site to KCTS Public Broadcast System, and our office sited the building in the interior open space created by the mounds.

Jordan Park (fka Everett Marina Park), Port of Everett, Everett, Washington (1972)

In 1970 the City of Everett Port Authority hired a contractor to dispose of approximately 9,000 cubic yards of dredged spoils from a yacht basin in the tidelands. The contractor wondered if the Seattle Center *modus operandi* could be repeated. The waste gave form to one of the earliest contemporary public earth sculptures, concurrent with Robert Smithson's *Spiral Jetty* and Robert Morris's *Observator*. A sequence of interlocking spaces on the ground plane are formed by multifaceted pyramids, with planes varying from one hundred percent to two percent. The Plaza Plane is a wind-shaded sun trap: The darkened concrete stores the sun's

Occidental Park, Jones & Jones, 1970, Seattle, Washington

warmth to fend off the evening coolness. The Morning Plane invites those who assemble to celebrate, to give witness, to party, and to play. The Great Pyramid rises to twenty-four feet, mothering her offspring. Set into her summit is a "secret" redoubt, the Watch Tower, a heightened expression—simultaneously—of the primal landscape values of prospect and refuge.

In 1990 I was informed by former students that there was a proposal to erase the earth forms and cover the site with asphalt. I personally orchestrated (from behind the scenes) a successful campaign to overturn the Port Commission's proposal. Question: Why are earthworks executed by landscape architects not held in as high esteem as similar works by sculptors?

The Redemption of Occidental Park, Seattle, Washington (1970)

The Pioneer Square Historic District, one of the best born-again assemblages of post-Victorian buildings, lies at the terminus of the original skid row. Nearby, a block of derelict buildings was razed to provide a parking lot. In 1970 Jones & Jones, architects and landscape architects, were commissioned to design Occidental Park on a half block of the parking lot. The park won an ASLA Merit Award for historic preservation and restoration. It was Seattle's first downtown "European" plaza. Occidental Park featured a shelter/bandstand that commanded a sun-washed square surrounded by a bosque of London plane trees. Many sturdy wooden benches were clustered over a cobbled pavement. The design was predicated on a rich program of performances, combined with retail- and food-vendor carts.

The mainstreaming of disadvantaged people, coupled with a declining economy and the clustering of volunteer social services, resulted in an increase of the numbers of "undesirable" people in the park. The surrounding merchants no longer supported the vendors and prevailed upon the park department "to do something to gentrify the park." The Seattle Park Department retained EDAW to do a survey and make recommendations. The recommendations were to: 1) remove shelter, 2) remove interior trees, 3) replace benches with removable plastic chairs, 4) replace or pave over cobblestones, and 5) plunk a great fountain in the center of the open space.

Although there was no funding for the new fountain, funding was found to begin dismantling Occidental Park. I assisted in forming Parks for People, an ad hoc committee of concerned citizens who organized a counteroffensive. The park was spared, hopefully for another twenty-five years. Only then will it be eligible to gain the Historic District protection.

Gas Works Park, Seattle, Washington (1968)

In 1906 a twenty-acre lakefront site was clear-cut. When coal and later oil were gasified, this noisy, noxious, toxic smokestack industry degraded the site, the lake, and its blue-collar dependents until the plant became obsolete (and benign) in 1955 with the introduction of natural gas. In 1969 I was commissioned to prepare a master plan. The genius loci suggested the importance of preserving the iron totems as a historic memorial to the Industrial Revolution. This controversial concept had to be sold to the skeptical community, and it became a hot political issue. The city council unanimously approved the master plan, and the legal document deeding the property to the city had to be redrafted to favor the plan.

Bioremediation techniques (nurturing the indigenous bacteria) were pioneered and successfully revivified the oil-soaked site in short order at minimal cost.

In 1981 Gas Works Park received the ASLA President's Award for Design Excellence (only one of many honors). In March 1984 the Environmental Protection Agency closed the park as a health hazard. In August 1984 a second opinion from a blue-ribbon task force of health-risk analysts gave the park a clean bill of health, and a huge reopening celebration marked the occasion.

Gas Works Park is secure as the foremost industrial fossil in the world. (Fourteen hundred such plants operated in the United States alone.) In 1994 the not-for-profit Friends of Gas Works Park (FoGWP) was established to foster the understanding and appreciation of the Park. It is FoGWP's goal to support the collection and translation of historical and educational information about the park into an exciting and thought-provoking form that will integrate with and enhance the existing park experience.

FoGWP's mission is twofold: to celebrate our industrial past, the technology, and the people behind it and to give new life to the totemic artifacts, true landmarks of Seattle's past, by utilizing one of the generator towers for the installation of a camera obscura.

In conclusion: Until recently I have been professing that the bond between human beings and Nature is immutable, that the spiral of life forces—the vast remembrance—is safely encoded in our genotype. Perhaps it is our gardens that must serve as more than mere metaphor to preserve "life, thought, and soul."

Richard Haag, FASLA, is a principal of Richard Haag Associates, Inc., Seattle, Washington, and a professor in the Department of Landscape Architecture, College of Architecture and Urban Planning, University of Washington.

Gas Works Park, Seattle, Washington.